Facilitator's Guide to

DIVERSITY IN THE CLASSROOM:
A CASEBOOK FOR TEACHERS AND TEACHER EDUCATORS

Amalia Mesa-Bains
and
Judith H. Shulman

of

The Far West Laboratory
for Educational Research and Development

Published collaboratively by Research for Better Schools and Lawrence Erlbaum Associates

Lawrence Erlbaum Associates, Inc., Publishers
365 Broadway
Hillsdale, New Jersey 07642

Library of Congress Cataloging-in-Publication Data

Facilitator's guide to Diversity in the classroom : a casebook for
  teachers and teacher educators / Amalia Mesa-Bains and Judith H.
  Shulman.
        p.   cm.
    Companion volume to Diversity in the classroom / edited by Judith
  H. Shulman and Amalia Mesa-Bains, 1993.
    ISBN 0-8058-1430-2 (pbk. : acid-free paper)
    1. Minorities--Education--United States--Case studies.
    2. Multicultural education--United States--Case studies.
    I. Shulman, Judith. II. Title. III. Title: Diversity in the
classroom.
    LC3731.M47 1994
    371.97'0973--dc20   94-7060
                                                           CIP

Work on this publication was supported in part by the U.S. Department of Education, Office of
Educational Research and Improvement, contract number RP91002006 and RP91002004. Its
contents do not necessarily reflect the views of the Department of Education.

Books published by Lawrence Erlbaum Associates are printed on acid-free paper, and their
bindings are chosen for strength and durability.

Printed in the United States of America

10 9 8 7 6 5 4 3 2 1

TABLE OF CONTENTS

INTRODUCTION

This guide is a companion volume to *Diversity in the Classroom: A Casebook for Teachers and Teacher Educators*, which presents 13 cases designed to help individuals and groups reflect on teaching. Specifically, the guide offers the information needed to use these cases in structured professional development experiences.

Teacher-written cases, depicting real-life problems other teachers are likely to face, can be powerful tools for reflection on practice. They can help teachers anticipate problems and solutions as they learn from others' real-life stories. Read alone, they offer the vicarious experience of walking in another's shoes. But in group discussion they are especially powerful, enabling differing points of view to be aired and examined.

Multiple and complex issues arise for teachers as the student population has become increasingly, sometimes enormously, mixed. This mix goes far beyond race. Diversity today refers to an array of races, cultures, and languages never before seen in single schools or classrooms. In these settings, issues stemming from class and gender take on different meanings. Majority-minority relations, once the focal concern in urban classrooms, may be moot, since in many schools there is no majority group. Or the dominant minority configuration, traditionally white-black, may instead be Latino-black or Chinese-Latino. Students' problems at home also profoundly influence what happens in the classroom — hardships faced by youngsters in urban housing projects, for example, or the struggles between generations in otherwise strong immigrant families.

Diversity in the Classroom addresses all of these concerns. Its teacher-authors describe in vivid detail their own successes and failures as they struggle with the complexities of teaching. Their compelling stories are excellent discussion catalysts, offering others the rare opportunity to analyze from a safe distance situations they, too, face.

Ultimately, knowledge gained from cases can provide the inspiration and provocation to change teaching behaviors. Often teachers have been reluctant to accept new cultural knowledge, not seeing its relevance to their effectiveness in the classroom. Cases help make that connection by describing abstract issues in concrete terms that mirror teachers' own experiences. Case discussion can lead teachers to examine their views, prejudices, and attitudes toward culturally diverse students and — as a result — begin to seek and use new teaching strategies.

Cases in this book focus on strategies for:

- initiating home contacts and fostering community relations;

- resolving cultural value differences between school and family;

- balancing personal involvement and cultural expectations;

- dealing effectively with immigrant and newcomer students;

- finding instructional strategies for multilingual classrooms;

- responding to at-risk students and disruptive situations; and

- understanding cultural issues involved in school site decision making and administration.

As you prepare to facilitate case discussion, a caveat is in order. Because these cases deal with highly sensitive topics not ordinarily addressed in teacher education programs, successful facilitating requires that you gain certain insights — not just into discussion-method teaching and its implied understanding of group dynamics, but also into techniques specific to discussing multicultural material.

Part I of this guide aims to equip you with such insights, particularly with strategies for deflecting hurtful confrontation or explosive interactions. In Part II — the main section — you'll find discussion notes for each case presented in *Diversity in the Classroom: A Casebook for Teachers and Teacher Educators* along with a suggested discussion outline. The appendices address interpersonal resistance and active learning.

Together, *Diversity in the Classroom* and this *Facilitator's Guide* can provide the content and structure for valuable experiences in reflective teaching. The facilitator should study both volumes before working with a group of teachers, and the group should have enough time allocated to reflect on the cases and share their own experiences. The result can be a powerful form of professional development.

PART I: FACILITATING A CASE DISCUSSION

Preparation and Process

Much can be learned just by reading cases. But a good facilitator can expedite that learning by prompting a group to examine the case's issues in ways that readers by themselves might not. Far more than a lecture, case discussion enlivens content and helps participants internalize theory. Still, the idea of facilitating such discussion can be intimidating: when you don't do all the talking, you relinquish authority and therefore can't be entirely sure how the class is going to go.

This concern is heightened when the issues at hand are emotionally provocative. In the pilot test of *Diversity in the Classroom* with groups of teachers, some of its cases, particularly those dealing with bias, race, and class, generated heated interchange and ran the risk of polarizing opinions and creating defensive attitudes. These topics can be talked about with candor and civility, however, and this section provides information to help ensure that this happens.

CONSTRUCTING A CASE-BASED PROFESSIONAL DEVELOPMENT CURRICULUM

Ideally, these case discussions don't take place in isolation; they are part of a case-based multicultural curriculum — a whole course or program built around the use of cases and including additional readings about the issues being addressed. Case discussion becomes more meaningful when supporting materials explain the general principles exemplified by the case. Conversely, the specific real people and situations detailed in each case put flesh and blood on otherwise nebulous concepts.

One of the biggest problems in multicultural education has been the tendency to deal in generalities; to talk of blacks, Latinos, Asians, or limited English speakers in terms of broad cultural characteristics. Professional development programs often teach cultural information,

human relations, or anti-racism. But without a specific situation for people to work their way through, the learning that takes place is disembodied and easily forgotten.

Cases, by contrast, can introduce an individual student, teacher, and classroom, bringing that world to life in all its complexity. Problems under discussion are no longer those of, say, poor black children, but of Eric — a very memorable, very real little boy with feelings, talents, and family members. His needs may or may not be "typical," but his teacher tries to meet them in the best way she and her school can. Teachers reading and discussing the case use this specific situation as a vehicle for questioning their own instructional practices, classroom management strategies, and multicultural curriculum and for reflecting on their own values, attitudes, and experience. Ideally information in the case is supplemented by other curriculum materials, e.g., a model that offers specific steps for handling disruptive classroom behavior or training in cooperative learning strategies; or material that raises important questions, such as why so many African-American boys are referred to special education. In other words, in a well-conceived curriculum the case functions as the hub of the staff development wheel.

Though reading or discussing a single case can be beneficial, it is the sustained use of cases in group discussion that spurs classroom change. A group generally needs to discuss at least four cases to acquire the comfort level, equity of participation, and analytical skills that allow discussion to move to more insightful levels. Moreover, the transfer of insights and cultural knowledge to the classroom doesn't really happen until reflective practices are internalized.

For each curriculum, case selection should be customized. In preservice, where participants have not yet tested themselves in the day-to-day life of the classroom, a varied group of cases giving insights into the world they are about to enter will be helpful. In the inservice environment, cases should have clear links to circumstances at participants' schools so that these teachers can compare the case experiences with their own. For example, if a school has a large number of limited English speaking students, "Then and Now: Insights Gained for Helping Children Learn English" and "Please, Not Another ESL Student" are likely candidates. Observations in the cases can lead teachers to identify specific areas, e.g., sheltered English, in which they want training.

Another way to bring cases closer to the school situation is to have participating teachers keep journals, jotting down observations about the cases that draw from their own classroom experiences. As part of a case-based curriculum, journals can become catalysts that move participants to begin writing their own cases.

An on-site, case-based professional development experience can have school-wide effects. Teacher isolation is reduced. Teachers who discover the strength in group problem solving may apply that process to other school issues, including deciding their own professional development needs. Since teachers of diverse backgrounds contribute special insights, their often marginalized status may change. For example, teachers of color may, for the first time, become truly integrated into their faculties.

PREPARING TO LEAD DISCUSSION

Careful preparation is critical to successfully leading case discussions. You'll need a thorough knowledge of the case and commentaries, as well as clear ideas about how best to use the commentaries and discussion notes to guide the sessions. The discussion notes in this guide frequently refer to material in the cases and commentaries which appear in *Diversity in the Classroom*.

Reading the case. To do a good job of facilitating discussion, one cardinal rule applies: you must have a good grasp of the case and its nuances. This is true for

any case, but especially crucial when delicate subject matter is involved. The only way to develop deep familiarity is to read the case many times over. The following suggestions can help:

- As you begin, take note of your first impression. What excites you? What bothers you? With whom did you relate? Subsequent readings may change your answers to these questions, so it's important to jot down those initial reactions to use as diagnostic tools. Initially, they help you gauge your own values and empathic response to the case. Later, they may be key in helping you understand participants' starting points for discussion.

- Since each case has many layers of meaning, each reading yields more information and understanding. As you read, ask yourself, "What is this a case of?" and "What are the different ways to interpret this case?" Also note the descriptive words, key phrases, and dialogue used, especially early in the case as the teacher-author introduces students or events. Often, these reveal the writer's racial and cultural perceptions, apprehensions, or hesitancies.

- You should also re-read the case with specific objectives in mind. For example, use one reading to identify teaching and learning issues; another to look for sociological impact (i.e., how will events described in the case affect this student's life in his or her community?) A third reading can focus on the teacher's role — what professional issues are at stake? The more perspectives you have on the case, the better equipped you'll be to prompt broad-ranging discussion, thus reinforcing the idea that there is no "one right answer," while also keeping group participation balanced. Should one person's viewpoint tend to dominate, your suggestion of another lens to look through can draw out participants whose knowledge and experience make them identify with the case in an entirely different way.

- Look for pressure or stress points in the case — instances when a teacher is confronted by angry students, puzzled by a dilemma, or experiencing doubt or remorse about his or her actions. In the discussion, these events can serve as teachable moments. For example, in "Moments of Truth: Teaching *Pygmalion*," a crisis is followed by a catharsis for teacher and students. If you can prompt teachers to explore different interpretations of this event, they may come to understand why the crisis occurred. This insight can help them avert a similar ordeal in their own classrooms.

- Look for subtle cues. Cases like "Fighting for Life in Third Period" overtly raise strong racial issues. But a real understanding of student and teacher actions requires examining the narrative's details, perhaps making paragraph-by-paragraph notations. In many of the cases, information about individuals' racial, cultural, and gender perspectives is couched in subtle details. To discern it you need to read between the lines, paying close attention to how the writer describes socio-economic, political, or historical features of students, communities, and families. Your goal is to continually try to elicit new cultural knowledge from the case that can help you and your group get beyond "is this or is this not a racist encounter?" — a discussion level that merely polarizes people. Instead, the group needs to look beneath the surface of what occurred. What might have happened if the teacher had perceived the student differently or known his or her culture well enough to really understand the meaning of gestures or behaviors? What might the teacher have done, and how might the student have responded?

Using the commentaries. The commentaries that follow each case can help you see these between-the-lines cultural indicators. Written by new and experienced teachers, administrators, teacher educators, and educational scholars, they offer multiple, often conflicting interpretations of the case. They are invaluable discussion aids, particularly when the group doesn't include a real cultural mix. The commentators then function as cultural informants, providing background essential to meaningful discussion, whether about realities of life in urban housing projects or the marginalization of minority teachers.

Besides adding information, the commentaries can help you prompt teachers to question their assumptions. The point of case discussion is to help teachers reflect on what they do and build on their prior knowledge. But to some degree, people are limited by what they already know. Your role includes helping participants expand their ways of thinking by investigating cultural complexities that may be outside their ken. The commentaries can help you shape questions that move things in this direction.

One clarification is in order here: the commentaries are not intended as verdicts that offer the "one best way" to interpret the case. On the contrary, one rationale for using cases is to provide a means of illustrating how complex teaching really is, thereby better preparing teachers for an ill-structured domain where there are few clear right or wrong courses of action. The commentaries for these cases aim to enrich the analysis by offering expert testimony, cultural witness, or counterpoints to ideas expressed in the case. They also enable you to speak with some level of cultural authority without purporting to have "the" answer and to change the direction of the discussion while maintaining neutrality as the facilitator.

How and when should you use the commentaries? Should they be read at the same time as the case? After case analysis so they don't preclude independent thought? There is no rule of thumb. Your decision depends on the individual case and your purpose in teaching it. It's true that discussing the case before reading the commentaries may preserve participants' original responses. But in some instances, reading the case and its commentaries together keeps the discussion from deteriorating into an opinion swap.

Experience suggests a caveat: for teachers at school sites, the commentaries may seem distant and over-intellectualized. Consequently, it may be advisable to have them read after discussing the cases. But, if you do so, be prepared to introduce them carefully. The risk is that participants may feel they've been set up for criticism, since the commentaries can appear to be judging the very opinions the group just expressed.

Using the discussion notes. The discussion outlines and notes in this guide are resources designed to help you plan each case discussion and gauge how to use the commentaries most effectively. As analytic interpretations, these notes may alert you in advance to potential problem areas. They examine key issues, particularly those dealing with race, culture, gender, and language, sometimes adding information that neither the case nor the commentaries include.

The discussion notes can also help you devise a structure for moving the group through the case. One common problem is that at certain points, discussion gets stuck. You introduce the case, set up questions, and analysis begins — but then stalls. Anticipating this, you can use the notes to identify stages of discussion and plan probes that will move things from stage to stage. Be aware, however, that the notes are not absolutes. There's no need to follow them step by step. Just as you customize case selection and sequence, you'll want to tailor questions to suit the profile of your particular group or school.

DYNAMICS OF THE GROUP PROCESS

For any discussion to succeed, a climate of trust is needed. Participants also need a sense of ownership — the outcome is theirs to determine. Clear ground rules must be established, and the facilitator has to be prepared to use gentle ways to quiet aggression and carry out his or her responsibility to protect (rather than control) the group.

Establishing trust. Successful case discussion can only take place in a climate of trust. How can you help ensure that participants feel safe enough to risk exposing their opinions to others' judgment?

You'll need to consider many factors: the physical setting, use of space, seating arrangement, your style of leading discussion, and group size. Perhaps most important in multicultural case discussions, however, is the life experience of group members. Each participant brings to the group his or her personal values, attitudes, and beliefs — both conscious and unconscious. Trust will be affected by unspoken concerns, fears of being perceived as racist, lack of cultural information, individuals' status in the group, histories at the school site, and even political agendas.

The clearer the structure and the more secure you are in the role of facilitator, the better the chances for a safe climate and productive discussion. Whenever possible, it helps to have culturally and racially balanced groups so that participants can learn from each other. But bear in mind that a balance in *participation* is a separate issue. People have different cultural values around communicating. Case discussion asks us to think about our responses to characters in the case. But often, how revealing people are willing to be about their values or beliefs is a function of their style of communication.

Some participants will find it easy to talk openly and debate the topics; others won't. Some will be aggressive; others will hold back until they hear the rest of the group's opinions. Some will want to speak first; others will need prodding to speak at all. Some will disagree openly; others indirectly. These styles reflect personality, but also culture. In classrooms we often subscribe to our own majority model — that you speak up when you disagree. But many ethnic groups don't feel that's appropriate.

So you need to create a cross-cultural climate. Partly, that means encouraging a variety of opinions through questioning and framing differing perspectives for examining the case. But it also means watching people's body language so you won't lose the chance when a quiet person is about to say something. You can step in and gently silence interrupters. ("Susan hasn't had a chance to share her ideas about the story, so let's give her that time.") See Appendix A for materials on dealing with interpersonal resistance.

Realistically, forming a culturally or racially balanced discussion group at a given site may not be possible. If the group is all of one background, whether Chinese, Latino, or white, it may be hard to introduce ways of thinking outside their experience. Another problem occurs when the group includes a lone minority member. That person is often cast in the role of expert witness. Others turn to him and say, "What do you think?" As the facilitator, you should consider in advance how to engage the rich knowledge and resources of that person's life experience without burdening him or her with naming solutions. Your sensitivity to the individual is critical. Some people are quite comfortable in the role of "cultural explainer." But many feel it shouldn't be their responsibility; racial and cultural issues should be everybody's business now.

In a group with well-established trust, the case discussion can provide the diverse participants a chance to reveal more of themselves and be better understood. In some instances a cultural catharsis can occur and must be handled delicately.

Finally, be aware that established roles among members of a given group may create an obstacle to open discussion because of people's fixed opinions about each other.

Rules and roles. We've already described some of the ground rules for discussion and roles played by the facilitator and participants. Here we summarize and elaborate on how you can establish a safe and supportive climate for discussion.

Case Discussion Goals. A first step is to ensure that participants understand the goals of a case seminar:

- To analyze and explore multiple interpretations of issues embedded in the case.

- To connect issues in the cases with participants' teaching situations and develop a repertoire of strategies to use in dealing with such issues.

- To improve understanding of multicultural issues — bias, race, class, ethnicity, and gender — that arise in classrooms and schools and enable teachers to reflect on their feelings about teaching diverse youngsters.

- To develop collegiality and a shared understanding among participants.

Ground Rules. Equally important, participants must overcome the notion that there is only one acceptable way to analyze each case. Instead, the aim is to foster an ethos of critical inquiry (see p. 9) that encourages multiple interpretations, conflicting opinions, and equal participation. Clear ground rules can help set the stage for this kind of discourse:

- Respect each member's contribution and point of view.

- Do not interrupt! Wait for speakers to finish their statements before responding.

- Do not let anyone monopolize the discussion. Provide equal opportunity for all members to contribute.

Role of the Facilitator. To support these ground rules, facilitators should:

- Ensure equal and full participation by keeping track of those who want to speak and making sure each has a chance.

- Encourage quiet members to contribute and tactfully redirect those who dominate.

- At suitable points, synthesize key ideas; help clarify those that are misunderstood.

- Model candor, courtesy, and respect, and remind participants of ground rules whenever necessary.

- Avoid being the "advisor" each time someone makes a comment. At times be a blank screen, giving others the opportunity to respond.

As we said earlier, in multicultural case-based seminars, facilitators must also engage participants in cross-cultural analysis. This goes back to the point that your goal is to continually elicit new cultural knowledge from the case. Achieving that goal means using the commentaries, the supportive participation of minority group members, or your questioning style to:

- Identify information in the details, setting, characterization, or dialogue in the case related to race, culture, class, language, or gender.

- Discuss all possible interracial or intercultural perceptions.

- Introduce specific cultural knowledge that has not voluntarily surfaced. (Use the commentaries or questions.)

- Go beyond acknowledging intercultural issues such as racism to analyze their forms, roots, and causes.

Leading the
Discussion

Remember that the group may need to get acquainted. Field testing showed that allowing time for participants to introduce themselves, or even using a simple icebreaker, sets a comfortable and warm climate and pays off later. If a group is going to meet several times, it may be worthwhile to use the first session just to get acquainted, go over rules and roles, and understand the purpose of cases.

Some of the practices suggested above at first may seem forced, but over time they become more comfortable. The facilitator's main job, of course, is to lead a substantive and constructive case discussion. Doing so requires knowing the cases well. It also means setting up a structure defining how you will open discussion, keep it moving, and end it. We noted earlier that the discussion notes — modified to suit your circumstances — can help you plan how to move through the case and involve as many interpretations as possible. Here are some further points to keep in mind.

THE OPENING

How do you begin discussion? Your opening questions are important; they set the tone and even the scope of the entire discussion. So, experimenting with ways to make your openings as flexible and participatory as possible should be one of your goals.

One approach is to establish the facts by asking one or two people to summarize what actually happened in the case, then asking others to join in. Another is to ask each participant to name one element he or she felt was significant in the case, then allow others to respond. The advantage here is that you get a good sense of the group's range of interpretations before discussion begins. You also convey the idea that there's more than one way to look at the case, thus helping ensure that discussion doesn't get fixated on a single view. (You may want to record these initial interpretations on newsprint so you can refer back to them at the end of the session.)

If the group is large enough, participants can pair up and briefly discuss the key issues (five minutes), then come back together to share important points they decided on. This makes for a dynamic beginning.

QUESTIONING TECHNIQUES

Besides knowledge of the narratives, your effectiveness relies on your repertoire of questioning techniques. Different types of questions (e.g., open-ended, diagnostic, challenging) can serve different purposes. A suggested question outline accompanies each discussion note. (See Appendix B for material on active listening.)

Remember, one sign of growth in the group is participants starting to ask questions of one another, rather than continually orienting their remarks toward you.

ETHOS OF INQUIRY AND CHANGING PRACTICE

One of the most important tasks of the facilitator is to create an ethos of inquiry — a group spirit that is not limited to exchanging opinions, but rather is creative, imaginative, and visionary enough to consider the entire universe of ideas. Accomplishing this task requires remembering that the focal point of a case discussion — the personalized narrative — can be both its hook and its pitfall. Its detailed, individual story draws people in. It prompts them to share their own stories, especially since they've often just left their own classrooms. But this level of discussion can be so absorbing that the group fails to realize that the point is to generate principles, or sets of practices, or new ways of thinking that can be tested across cases.

The facilitator's challenge is, first, to build an ample world of ideas for the group to explore, then to move discussion up and down a ladder of exploration: up to higher principles, back down to very discrete practices, then up again. In other words, to repeatedly move from the level of opinion swap to the desired level of applied knowledge. How do you do that? How do you get people to deduce principles from experiences they're discussing? To go away, come back, then generalize again?

- Use the commentaries. As stated earlier, they amplify ideas put forth in the case and afford the group more grist for discussion.

- Try not to get emotionally involved in what's being said. You will be more effective if you keep some distance and continually analyze how the discussion is going. Pay particular attention to equitable participation.

- Think of the discussion as incremental. For each increment, ask questions in a sequence that moves the group back to a critical point, i.e., rather than just preparing questions, develop probes or variations on a question. For example, when a group discussing "From Outsider to Active Learner" began to digress on the perils of modern society, MTV, and drugs, the facilitator refocused by asking, "How might a newcomer face such an overwhelming change from his or her traditional culture?" "How would parents help?" "How can the teacher help student and family bridge cultural differences?" Questioning can elicit strategies that might have resolved the case. This approach can inspire teachers to try to make changes in their own situations.

- Periodically tie up loose ends, summarize what's been learned, and move along to the next increment. This keeps the group from repeatedly coming back to the same point or spreading out so far that their talk no longer has anything to do with the case.

- Bear in mind that you are teaching the skills of case analysis. Ultimately, you are moving participants toward applying what they're learning to their teaching behaviors. But only in-depth analysis allows that learning to occur, and the skills required take time to develop.

The possibility of a true ethos of inquiry is much enhanced if you structure a case-based curriculum. As explained above, this involves assigning other readings that play off the commentaries and expand on cultural knowledge or appropriate classroom strategies. When discussion takes place in such a structure, the group will not be confined to talking only about what they think happened in the narrative or their personal values or beliefs, but can explore other people's ways of looking at a given topic.

Your larger goal is to extend this approach beyond the single case discussion to the entire multicultural course or curriculum. Over time, discussion will have covered a family of cases, which then can be criss-crossed, or compared with each other. At the end, you should be able to engage participants in framing guiding principles that they now feel would apply, not just to teaching inner city kids like the individuals in the cases, but to any teaching in diverse settings where issues such as language, gender, class, and race come into play.

The greatest challenge of the case approach is that each discussion is different and takes on a life of its own. Your role is not to indoctrinate, but to provoke, inform, and provide equal opportunities to contribute. This is sometimes easier said than done, however. (See "Discussion Stages and Struggles" on p. 13.) At times, the discussion may appear at an impasse. Or participants may be ignoring information you feel is key to understanding the case's cultural issues. At such times, you need to shift the topic. One way of doing so is to say you're going to play devil's advocate, then introduce the missing issue as a counterpoint. Or you might quote from the case or commentaries and raise questions about the quote. Yet another tack, if it fits in comfortably, is to give a two- or three-minute *mini*-lecture based on the commentaries, teaching notes, or other scholarly articles. (This can be risky, however, if perceived as too directive. It may also serve to limit discussion.) A third is to incorporate activities such as role-playing and/or structured small groups, which can offer a welcome change of pace. Ultimately, we are trying to move participants from reflection to problem solving and a willingness to change their own classroom practice.

CLOSING THE CASE DISCUSSION

Another major challenge is helping participants synthesize and reflect on what they learned from the entire discussion. Participants should have the opportunity to identify new understandings as well as unresolved conflicts and questions.

One approach is to ask them to spend a few minutes writing answers to questions such as: What new insights did you gain from the case discussion? Do you have lingering questions? What part of the discussion did you find most challenging? How can you relate what we discussed to your own experience? What strategies could the teacher have used? Another is to divide the group into pairs to share what they learned, relate it to their own experience, and brainstorm what they would now do differently. After the pairs meet, bring the group back together and ask one member of each pair to report key ideas they discussed. A third tactic is simply to go around the group asking participants to state insights or understandings. Record this information; perhaps compare it with the group's initial analysis.

Some facilitators who use cases throughout a semester urge participants to keep a journal in which they record insights and questions regarding the case; reflections on their own practices (a form of case writing) to be shared with the group later in the term; and strategies they have found to be successful in diverse settings.

Discussion Stages and Struggles

No group achieves a climate of trust without a series of struggles. Facilitators need to be aware that groups undergo developmental growth. Along the way, people shift roles and become more at ease with differences of opinion. Part of your job is to create a nonjudgmental climate that supports this progression.

The group's comfort level is directly related to your own. As your skills develop, your confidence grows and your anxieties diminish. Your equanimity then sets a tone supportive of people whose opinions may strongly differ from yours. Providing informal opportunities for socializing also helps establish warmth that carries over into the discussions.

Once established, a climate of trust may lead a group member to make a personal revelation in the course of explaining his or her reaction to a case. Such moments can be fragile; your support and the respect of the group are crucial. Such moments can also be breakthroughs, moving the group to a deeper level of discussion and creating strong group bonds.

We noted earlier that people participate in different ways, and their participation may be related to racial and ethnic perceptions and roles. As the facilitator, you play a strong role in determining who dominates the discussion or who is not contributing. Take the time to examine that role. Doing so requires a sort of self-diagnosis, using questions analogous to those you used in your search for meaning in the case. Immediately after reading the case, you asked, "What did I feel about the story? What did I really like or not like?" Now you should step back and ask, "To whom do I find myself asking questions? Do I have favorites?"

White members of the group, particularly men, often dominate the discussion and overshadow others. If you are white, you may not notice this unless you consciously look for it. You may also need to ask yourself if you tend to support the white participants more than

others — not because you are prejudiced, but because your frame of reference and theirs are probably similar. People of color may react to elements of the case in ways that are alien to you. They may sense things you don't sense, and that disparity may be unbalancing for you at first.

Conversely, if you are a person of color, you may notice that you are more comfortable supporting participants of color and their views.

Recognize that on some level, cultural and racial experiences, values, and behaviors will affect the way people communicate and the way they perceive communication. For example, we mentioned earlier that people differ in their willingness to make direct statements. When you get to the point in discussion where the ethos of inquiry requires critiquing things in the case — stating what you identify with, agree or disagree with — often black and white members of the group will take far more active roles than, say, Latinos or Asians, who are not necessarily as comfortable with direct statements that might be viewed as judgmental or harsh. These are generalizations to be sure, but they help make the point: it's critical to examine the racial issues in communication for yourself and your group.

As the facilitator, be aware of how your own style of communicating influences your responses to participants' behaviors: Who do you feel is getting carried away and who do you feel comfortable with? Your responses allow or impede productive discourse. In short, your best diagnostic tool for knowing whether the group is progressing toward nonjudgmental discourse is your own comfort level.

The discussion offers the potential to gain insights into more effective teaching with diverse students. But that potential can only be realized through the group's process of reflection. If successful, the group may become a microcosm of what we're trying to accomplish in a multicultural society: to reach a place where inquiry, reflection, and respect are the norm, fostering trust and equal participation.

Case 1

A Case of Ganas

Ganas, the Spanish word for desire or will, is an appropriate title for this story of Amparo, an earnest Mexican-American girl struggling to write. Amparo's efforts are matched by the dedication of her teacher, who is well aware of this student's expressive problems. The teacher's dilemma is that she wants to respect Amparo's wish to compete in a writing contest, but she realizes how much of her own time it will take to provide individualized support, proofreading, and corrections. Amparo's touching family story and the implications of her Spanish-speaking background raise cultural and linguistic questions about this student. But the dominant theme seems to be the teacher's frustration and her feeling that she failed to help Amparo make a real breakthrough.

CONTEXT

Like many other Mexican-American students living in the Southwest, Amparo's learning is affected by her people's historic experience with disenfranchisement and discrimination. We know little of her own family's immigrant history, but the case indicates she is part of a sizeable Chicano community whose residents often live in barrios. Youngsters like Amparo struggle with bilingualism and bi-culturalism. Given appropriate support, students can turn this social challenge into a creative force. But at school their language status is often poorly assessed. And at home, despite a strong culture of support, family members are dealing with their own lack of schooling and second language skills. These problems combine with economic and social concerns to make it doubly hard for barrio students to stay in school.

Amparo's *ganas*, or desire, is remarkable when we consider the obstacles she faces. The teacher doesn't seem to recognize the pattern of errors in the writing or that such a pattern may be a product of her Spanish-speaking background. Moreover, Amparo's schooling history is vague, little seems known about her learning problems, and she misses the class screening. Despite her long-time U.S. residency, it is possible that she is part of a growing number of English-Dominant-Language-Minority (EDLM) students — students who have not mastered English structures, yet no longer can be expressive or literate in their first language. Though socially fluent in English, such students often mix languages and have serious problems with comprehension and writing. This condition can exist for several generations in a family, particularly when schools lack strong bilingual programs.

Often, EDLM students don't qualify for bilingual services. With little or no recognition of their problems, they fall between the cracks. Their superficial English lacks the deep constructs of English mastery that allow more complex use of English in problem solving, contextual reading, and interpretive expression. Consequently, these students are excluded from the more linguistically sophisticated exchanges that take place in the classroom.

Amparo's problems with "gibberish" in her writing may in fact be the result of her English-as-a-second-language transfer from Spanish, coupled with some learning disabilities. We know from her writing that in her other school she was once in a "special class." How to interpret this information is another matter. The Mexican American Legal Defense Fund has documented that large numbers of Spanish-speaking children are placed in special education classes even though they've never been assessed in their own language. (Schools lacking Spanish-language assessments tend to fall back on testing these children in English.) Some of these students do not have learning disabilities. Others, like Amparo, may have real special education needs that will go unmet because no sufficient assessment is available to identify them.

Without such assessments, and lacking bilingual support and an understanding of EDLM, students like Amparo struggle alone against tremendous odds to express themselves.

SEGMENTS OF THE DISCUSSION

This discussion must consider both the teacher's and the student's needs. Participants should be encouraged to share their own knowledge of writing and second language issues.

What do we know about the teacher? It's evident that the teacher is willing to put in extra time to support her students' special needs. But her attempts to help Amparo are hampered by her lack of knowledge about this student's learning problems and her apparent feeling that the only way to work with Amparo is one-to-one.

As the teacher describes her demanding role as Amparo's sole editor and support person, we see that her writing model doesn't include peer strategies. She is also extremely concerned with grammatical and spelling errors. While we know that the competition requires correct presentation, we can't help but wonder why in the earlier stages she doesn't encourage peer pairing and strategies of creative writing. Even the retitling of Amparo's essay indicates problems in instructional approach, despite the teacher's good intentions. More commonly, creative writing teachers use a more open and correction-free approach when beginning work with limited-English proficient students. Discussion participants should be encouraged to brainstorm alternative models for this challenging task.

There are also questions about how much the teacher controlled the nature of Amparo's writing. The change in title and focus in the writing about her family may tell us more about the teacher's expectations than about what the student wanted to say. Despite her references to Amparo's potential learning problems, we find the teacher reverting to talk of "serious mechanical problems" and "gibberish," which suggests she lacked understanding. Could she have sought help for Amparo from a bilingual teacher? Could she have responded to Amparo with another kind of support besides editing?

What do we know about the student? This young student demonstrates a creative will to succeed despite a difficult situation. Her desire to enter the contest indicates a need to excel and produce. Yet we feel that something else drives her to write. It's as if the writing itself helps her make sense of what is happening to her. Struggling as all adolescents do with her own identity, she perhaps uses the writing to explain herself. In the epilogue, for example, she reveals a coming-of-age as she describes her "presentation" or *quinceañera*, the coming-out party for 15-year-olds common in Mexican communities. At the same time, we learn of her sense of inadequacy at her other school when she was in a "special class." Like many girls her age, she balances her feelings of young womanhood with her concerns about her competency and worth.

Amparo's reflections — like a story within a story — also present to us a strong cultural identity rooted in shared family values. We are reminded of the primacy given to family life and the role of the father among many Mexican families, and we see the kinds of expectations held for girls. There is a wisdom to Amparo's thoughts about her family, their roles, and her neighborhood. Yet the teacher seems to center on the problems she finds in Amparo's writing process itself. Could the teacher have responded to Amparo's writing differently? What was Amparo trying to achieve with her writing?

The language riddle. Throughout the narrative, the teacher focuses on mechanical errors and seems consumed with the notion that Amparo's ability to improve is at best limited. She begins her story by stating that Amparo wasn't even following phonetic patterns of sound in her spelling, as though some sign of phonetic spelling would indicate potential for remediation.

Instead, it was all "gibberish." But upon closer examination, Amparo's spelling is phonetic — Spanish phonetics applied to English. In the epilogue passages there are consistent vowels, consonants, and consonant endings characteristic of the Spanish language. The B for V transposition permissible in Spanish is apparent in the word "faborit" (favorite). And Amparo's sentence structure is understandable considering that Spanish allows for modifiers and adverbial clauses that produce what we would call run-on sentences.

Amparo's writing shows the bilingual speaker's tendency to transpose Spanish language syntax and structure into English language usage. Had more linguistic information been available to the teacher, her very first impression, and perhaps her expectations of Amparo, might have been quite different.

CLOSING THE DISCUSSION

The story impresses readers with Amparo's tenacity and the teacher's endurance. Before closing the discussion, ask the participants to examine alternatives for working with Amparo. How might teacher and student have worked together more effectively?

SUGGESTED DISCUSSION OUTLINE

1. What were the major language and culture issues in the case?

2. After the issues are raised, what further information must be considered?

   Probes:

   a. What is known about Amparo's background?

   b. What were the teacher's reasons for approaching support of this student as she did?

   c. What were the teacher's expectations of Amparo? Why?

3. What were the teacher's perceptions of the student?

   Probes:

   a. How did she see the language problems?

   b. What did she know about Amparo?

   c. What else would she have needed to know?

   d. What were the teacher's needs?

   e. What might have happened if she had sought bilingual help?

4. What does the case tell us about the cultural setting?

   Probes:

   a. What are the language issues for Amparo and her family?

   b. What does Amparo's paper tell us about her hopes and dreams?

   c. What do we know about other Mexican-American students that might pertain to Amparo's situation?

   d. What are some of the issues for teaching writing to LEPs?

   e. What was Amparo trying to achieve with her writing?

5. How might this teacher have dealt with other ways to assist Amparo in her writing?

Probes:

    a.   What other models exist for creative writing?

    b.   Would peer strategies have worked?

    c.   What would the risks and consequences have been to using new strategies?

    d.   Using Kawazoe's commentary, what could the teacher have done differently?

6.   What does the epilogue convey?

Probes:

    a.   About Amparo?

    b.   About the teacher?

7.   What can be learned from Amparo's story?

Probes:

    a.   What are some guiding principles?

    b.   What cultural knowledge was gained?

Moments of Truth: Teaching Pygmalion

The case begins with a veteran teacher from an urban high school presenting a lesson on George Bernard Shaw's *Pygmalion* to her English class. Though she is sure she has confronted her own racial discomforts, we find that this teacher is anxious. She wants to maintain an impersonal context for her largely non-white students from poor communities while teaching *Pygmalion*'s themes of social inequality, perceptions of appearances, and personal identity. But she anticipates that students may find the lesson offensive.

In class, her worries prove well founded. Students challenge her for using references to their personal backgrounds and neighborhoods in a way they find insensitive. So, the teacher faces the very thing she sought to avoid: confrontation. In fact, she is confronted by a student she finds menacing. It is ironic that help comes from another student.

This case deals with a teacher's response to confrontation, her students' involvement in that response, and broader issues of curricula, cultural sensitivity, and relevance. Ultimately, the case focuses on how a teacher should deal with powerful student realities. Should she try to avoid or enlist them? The teacher's conclusions about her experience leave us with many questions. The commentaries prompt thoughts about missed opportunities and race/class issues in the learning situation.

(**Caution:** This case is quite complex, it might be best used toward the end.)

Context

Though she has taught in the same inner-city high school for over eight years, this Anglo teacher is still hesitant about dealing with racial issues. She grew up in a rural, mainly white area. The students she describes are urban, poor, and 85 percent non-white. She perceives them as having deficient home environments and believes that she can help make up for some of those deficits.

Perhaps one of the most telling aspects of the disparity between the teacher's idealism and the students' realism is her early belief that she is color blind, oblivious to student race. Her later recognition of her own racism seems to enable change. By the end of the case, her shifting realizations about race are seen to affect the classroom lesson.

Segments of the Discussion

The important role interpersonal relations play in instruction requires a look at the differences between the teacher's and students' beliefs and experiences. What were some of the vulnerable points in the teaching of *Pygmalion* because of such differences? What were the critical incidents in the teaching of the lesson? Could they have been handled differently? Could the teacher have drawn upon the students' reality rather than trying to distance it from her lesson?

What do we know about the teacher? The teacher alternately reveals color blindness and prejudice. She acknowledges earlier discomforts with black students, but regards them as resolved. Yet her extreme preparation, sleepless nights, and fear of conflict might indicate otherwise. She tries to use the curriculum guide and the popular film version, *My Fair Lady*, to help her make Shaw's play more relevant. Clearly, this teacher is willing to work hard at drawing her students into the lesson.

But her recognition of race and class differences brings her struggle to the surface. She is concerned that the students' reality is too far discrepant from the setting of *Pygmalion*, even as its themes may be too close and perhaps offensive. Her fear of conflict guides her decisions on the thematic application of the lesson. She feels that the material is inappropriate, yet she tries to draw relevance for her students. She acknowledges that language is a problem, but fails to note the real complexity for black students well acquainted with language discrimination.

What do we know about the students? These students live at the poverty level. Every day they deal with harsh realities. As urban blacks, they may also speak nonstandard English. They are aware of class differences between the poor and the middle-class. All this in mind, what associations could students be making as the teacher asks her study questions: "Why do you think people often base their impressions of others on the way they speak? What is the contrast between upper and lower classes in the play? What is the relationship between class and language, the way a person speaks, and his or her identity?"

The students' world offers the teacher a rich basis for extending the lesson and helping the students deal with the inequities of which they are so well aware. How could these questions have been linked to students' experiences, so they could relate to them without being offended?

The use of the classic. Teaching classic literature in today's multicultural urban schools is a challenge for teachers concerned with life-relevant curriculum. This teacher's difficulties with *Pygmalion* demonstrates why many are seeking more culturally diverse textbooks and sensitive instructional practices for the inner-city classroom. Great controversy surrounds this issue. Educators are struggling to find a curriculum that blends both Western and non-Western contributions. In this case, could George Bernard Shaw's classic have offered an opportunity to approach both diversity and Western literature together?

In such a culturally diverse setting, the teacher's attempt to make an English classic approachable turns out to be a complex undertaking. Ultimately, the teacher relies on the concepts in the curriculum guide, while attempting to use the film as an entry point that is more understandable. Unfortunately, the film does not emphasize the satire so key to Shaw's biting critique of England's class issues, and therefore does not help the teacher prepare the students to bridge their community issues with the setting in the play. *Pygmalion* offers a vehicle for relating contemporary issues facing urban students to similar concerns from another period of history. Shaw's satire examines the British upper classes and the cockney-speaking underclass through the story of a professor refashioning the belligerent flower girl, Eliza. The professor's high-handed attempts to refine Eliza's language and behavior bring up questions of social equality and appearances.

These three key ideas — social equality, appearances, and identity — are significant to the students in this class. It is important to remember that adolescents are forming their personal and social identities. They are self-conscious, easily embarrassed, and hypersensitive to injustice. For racially and culturally diverse adolescents, *Pygmalion*'s themes are even more delicate.

By not providing a forum for exploring these ideas in a way that relates to these students' lives, the teacher may have inadvertently caused the confrontation she most feared. She didn't realize how powerful her students' beliefs and experiences were and only touched upon them through her questions about the character Eliza. Commentator Gloria Ladson-Billings remarks on this misapplication of the themes and the teacher's missed opportunity. Karen Desser's commentary takes the issue of black language further and even suggests student activities, while providing a bibliography for teacher knowledge.

The retrospective view. The teacher's honesty and directness in handling the confrontation is effective, but her reflections are troubling. She comes to some conclusions about future use of the film and key ideas, but her assessment of the students is still flawed. She wants to avoid having the students identify personally with the characters; paradoxically, she plans to explore the social themes and how they relate to the students' lives. Her beliefs about honest communication seem at odds with her fear of personalizing.

How could she use the students' personal context to move them toward using the play to examine their own critical issues? How could she come to terms with their creative language and the language discrimination so thematic to the story? Could she begin with the same key ideas but present them differently to ready the students for the play? How could she use this classic play to help them see how other societies throughout history have dealt with these issues of class, discrimination, and change?

CLOSING THE DISCUSSION

This encounter of student experience, teacher expectation, and a mandated curriculum capsulizes the challenge of urban education. There are many ways the teacher could have proceeded, and the discussion should allow for all the options.

SUGGESTED DISCUSSION OUTLINE

1. What are the key elements in this case?

2. What is the significance of the beginning encounter with a student who asks the teacher, "How does it feel to be a minority?"

   Probes:

   a. What was the student really saying?

   b. What do we learn from the teacher's response? What were her biases?

   c. Why do you think she began the story here?

3. What was the teacher's chief concern in teaching *Pygmalion*?

   Probes:

   a. What was she anxious about?

   b. Why did she decide to create an impersonal context?

   c. What were the pros and cons of using the curriculum guide and the film?

4. How about the moment of confrontation, when the student challenged the teacher to present her neighborhood?

   Probes:

   a. What leads up to it?

   b. How could the teacher have handled it?

   c. What would have been the risks and consequences?

   d. What were the students trying to tell her?

   e. What did she fail to understand? (See Ladson-Billings' commentary on the distance between the students' lives and the teacher's.)

5. What about the students' point of view?

   Probes:

   a. How do you think they would have wanted *Pygmalion* to be taught?

   b. How could their experience have been bridged to the characters in the play?

   c. What do you think was the most compelling part of the play?

   d. What kind of activity could have prepared the students to begin the play?

e.   Discuss Desser's commentary on alternative instructional practices and the concept of cultural dominance.

6.   If we were going to rewrite the ending of the story, what would be our conclusion?

Probes:

a.   Do you agree or disagree with the teacher's conclusions?

b.   Did she understand the issues of relevancy, impersonal teaching, and differentiating from characters?

c.   What was the teacher's confusion?

7.   What did you learn from this case?

Probes:

a.   What principles would you consider when teaching classic literature to diverse learners?

b.   What principles would you consider when preparing a lesson for difficult situations?

Case 3

Attempting to Teach Self-Esteem

This case is about a third grade teacher's unsuccessful attempt to create a lesson that would raise her inner-city students' sense of self worth. The activity involved a self-discovery lesson with a mirror and a guessing game, during which each child was supposed to realize that he or she was "a very important person." But the youngsters didn't get the point. What went wrong? Why weren't the children able to relate the teacher's questions about important people to themselves? Does telling children that they are important help them believe it?

Readings on the developmental stages of growth (e.g., Piaget) would provide a useful theoretical context for analyzing this case. Amalia Mesa-Bains refers to such theories in her commentary. Peg Foley Reynolds, a teacher who tries other approaches to raise her students' self-esteem, offers a practical perspective on what went wrong.

CONTEXT

This case takes place in an ethnically diverse, inner-city school. Most of the students come from single-parent, low-income families who live in housing projects. The teacher-author notes that her class reflects "the struggles of young, mostly immigrant families, trying to survive in today's big city." As the daughter of Asian immigrants herself, the teacher strongly identifies with their plight.

SEGMENTS OF THE DISCUSSION

Facilitators may want to frame this session around how the developmental stages of growth influence learning. After reviewing the developmental stages, ask if this lesson appears to be developmentally appropriate for third graders. Why or why not? What were the teacher's goals for the lesson? What actually happened? How did the children respond?

What do we know about the teacher? Even from the meager description about her background, we can

hypothesize that this teacher cares a great deal about the students in her class. "I was sick of seeing students with low self-esteem, and I wanted so badly to do something about it," she writes. She tries to find out about their home life. For example, she knows that Nathan, the child selected to take the first peek in the mystery box, was "the oldest of four boys from a modest home."

We can also hypothesize that this teacher constantly reflects on her teaching — trying to understand why some lessons are more successful than others. Though she initially blamed her failure on her student's deficiencies, such as limited English or difficult family situations, she also took responsibility for her lack of success. Evidence of this is her search for help from her principal and peers as she retraced what happened. When she tried the lesson again, she was both more prepared for their reactions and more realistic about how much she could accomplish in a single lesson.

What do we know about the students? As noted above, most of the students come from single-parent, low-income families who live in project housing; many of the families have recently immigrated to this country. At what developmental stage are these children? Mesa-Bains points out in her commentary that these students can grasp concrete ideas, but they generally cannot understand abstract concepts. In this particular lesson, the students appear to be in a transition stage. Though they can relate the concept of "importance" to influential adults, they cannot relate it to themselves. Clearly they do not believe that their importance can be compared to that of more famous persons.

Analysis of the lesson. Is this lesson appropriate for third graders? How useful was the direct approach? Mesa-Bains notes that providing opportunities for experiencing competence and independence might contribute more to the students' sense of self-worth than trying to help the students perceive their importance. Foley Reynolds also questions in her commentary whether the students have enough English understanding and background knowledge to make this lesson meaningful. She offers an alternative approach.

Perhaps this teacher provided follow-up activities on this topic during the year, because it appears that at least one student, Denise, demonstrated knowledge of the objectives in her journal entry.

What are some alternate approaches to improving students' self esteem? What are the risks and consequences for each? This would be a good opportunity for participants to share their own experiences.

CLOSING THE DISCUSSION

Facilitators should provide an opportunity for participants to synthesize what they have learned. Perhaps they can generalize some principles for assessing whether a particular lesson appears developmentally appropriate and meaningful for particular groups of students.

SUGGESTED DISCUSSION OUTLINE

1. What were the facts of this case?

    Probes:

    a. What were the teacher's objectives for the lesson?

    b. What actually happened?

    c. How did the teacher feel about the failure of her lesson?

    d. What did she do about it?

2. What do we know about this teacher?

Probes:

a. Ethnic background?

b. Caring for students?

c. Reflection on her teaching?

3. What do we know about the students?

    Probes:

    a. Ethnic diversity?

    b. Socio-economic backgrounds?

    c. Developmental level of understanding?

    d. How do you think the students viewed this lesson?

4. Why did the lesson initially fail?

    Probes:

    a. Developmental level of the students?

    b. Lack of preparation activities that would enable them to experience success and a sense of importance?

5. What alternate strategies could the teacher have tried to teach this concept?

    Probes:

    a. What are the risks and consequences for each strategy?

    b. What evidence can you give that each suggested strategy is more developmentally suitable?

6. Do you agree that "improving self-worth" is an appropriate concept to teach young children?

   Probe:

   a. Why or why not?

   b. Should we assume that these children have low self-esteem (see commentary by Amado Padilla in Case 9: "A Trip to Hell")?

7. How would you/have you handled similar lessons?

   Probes:

   a. Were your lessons successful? Why?

   b. What are the risks and consequences of your strategies?

   c. What strategies have you seen or read about that you think are noteworthy to explore?

8. What principles can we generate from this case discussion?

Then and Now: Insights Gained for Helping Children Learn English

In this case a teacher compares a long-ago "painful failure" at teaching a non-English-speaking student with her much more gratifying experience in a similar situation years later. During her first year of teaching, Magnus, a sixth grader, arrives from Norway mid-year. With no district support and no special training, the teacher tries to help him but has little success. Knowing something is wrong, she takes her concerns to his parents. But they don't see a problem. They believe Magnus's shyness explains his language and social underdevelopment. Later, with the advantage of hindsight, the teacher blames such factors as traditional seating and lack of cooperative models for Magnus's isolation and hindered capacity to learn English.

Twenty-five years later, the teacher has acquired both district support and expertise in working with non-English-speaking students. Her third-grade class currently includes a girl from Korea whose family recently immigrated to this country. We immediately notice several elements different from the situation with Magnus. First, the parents insist that the teacher use the student's new American name, Sandy, and not her given Korean name. An interpreter is also present, and student grouping and student assistance have been designed to help non-English speakers. Moreover, the teacher uses specific strategies to help Sandy learn English. The "isolation" Magnus experienced does not happen for Sandy.

Context

Back when this teacher met Magnus, little was known about how to integrate non-English speakers into schools and classrooms. Many of the ESL and bilingual scholars were just then beginning to write up their research.

Magnus's situation involves a set of aspirations, expectations, and attitudes atypical of the problem. He only came to this country for a short time and apparently had little motivation to integrate into American society. He was coping with a new situation and had left friends behind. His distress, normal under these circumstances

for children his age, could explain his low affect, isolation, and lack of interaction, yet the teacher blames the traditional classroom setting. Even her comparison to his younger sibling is problematic. At Magnus's brother's age, language acquisition and socialization are much easier.

Sandy's story 25 years later involves a very different set of motivations and supports. Unlike the Norwegians, Sandy's family is here permanently. Her parents are eager to make a new life in the U.S., a critical motivator for acquiring new customs and a new language. Moreover, their extended Korean-American community helped strengthen the cultural bridge between home and school. The commentary by Lois Meyer sheds light on these issues and can be used to trigger discussion of them.

Segments of the Discussion

What do we know about the teacher? As a novice, this teacher felt profoundly isolated. In retrospect, she realizes that her classroom's lack of cooperative support for the student mirrored her own lack of support as a new teacher. She readily acknowledges the absence of ESL support services and describes with frustration her attempts to help Magnus with English. At the same time, however, she is able to accept his success in mathematics as evidence of some school achievement. Like many beginning teachers, she chooses not to voice her concerns, even when she notes how well Magnus's kindergarten brother learned English. Rather, she harbors her feelings of inadequacy in silence. With hindsight, the teacher concludes that student involvement and an interactive environment are necessary to natural oral language development.

By the time Sandy is in her class, the teacher speaks knowledgeably of the natural approach to second language acquisition. This approach takes into account the stages of reception and production that develop from listening and interacting in a rich classroom situation rather than through the traditional methods of isolated drill and practice. The teacher's awareness of spontaneous production indicates that the student is not being forced into premature speaking by unrealistic demands. This respect for the student's own development is also a key. The relationship between literacy in her native language and oral language development is taken into consideration because it assures the teacher that basic skills can be more easily transferred across languages.

The years of teaching in support of ESL have given this teacher a broad knowledge of key concepts such as comprehensible input. She recognizes that instructional and socially supportive approaches will help the new student understand the activities and experiences in the classroom.

What do we know about the students? Magnus is a white, Norwegian sixth grader who arrives mid-year. His father is in a business that allows him to relocate his entire family for six months and then return to his native country. Both parents speak English. Magnus spends most of his time in isolation, making no friends in school and learning only limited English. Nonetheless, his mother feels that he is happy and comfortable in school, and attributes his isolation to shyness.

Sandy is an immigrant Korean third grader whose non-English-speaking parents seek to both build a life in the new country and make ties with the local Korean-American community. These differences in status and motivation to learn may affect Sandy's desire and capacity to learn English. Moreover, unlike Magnus, she is still in an early stage of natural oral development and has not yet contended with the social peer pressure of beginning adolescence. Thus Sandy is more flexible, receptive, and language-ready than Magnus. Meyer's commentary is a very helpful resource for examining all of these issues.

Sandy's situation and needs are characteristic of Asian newcomer students. She is adjusting to U.S. society and also to the historic Asian-American community here.

Such students bring to the classroom both a bi-cultural and a second language challenge. Pairing Sandy with a Korean-American student supports her on both fronts at an age when such support will have great impact.

ESL instruction. Facilitators may want to use this case discussion as an opportunity to begin examining effective ways to integrate non-English speakers into classrooms. What are some things to consider? What techniques did this teacher use during her first year? What was effective? What other things could she have considered? Compare the first experience to the second. What was different?

In the first instance, the teacher knew little about bilingual education, so she was forced to use a trial-and-error approach to teach Magnus English. She had none of the visual or auditory materials used today and didn't know about sheltered English techniques such as body and facial expressions, hand gestures, voice queuing, repetition, and the use of objects — all common in today's bilingual classrooms. She also did not know about the natural approach to language acquisition, which would have helped her appreciate that language production must come at its own speed. It makes sense that a sixth grade boy in a new social setting where he is the only non-English speaker may be hesitant to speak for fear of error and embarrassment. Age, gender, and context are all factors in acquiring a second language.

In reflecting about Magnus, the teacher acknowledges some of the issues that have affected her current methods of ESL instruction. Her understanding of the natural development of oral language assists her in realizing the importance of student interaction, group activities, and supportive materials.

By the time Sandy arrives, the school has formal ESL classes, one hour per week, supplemented by volunteers for individualized instruction. The teacher's increased knowledge is apparent in her consideration of Sandy's native language literacy and its relationship to her oral language development. Her description of Total Physical Response Methods, an established ESL technique, and also her observation about spontaneous production in natural language development, reveal the teacher's expertise. She now uses a variety of curriculum materials, auditory aids, language activities, and socialization opportunities to help the students. In fact, her recognition of the relationship of socialization to second language acquisition has become her greatest teaching asset.

As we note this teacher's increase in understanding ESL strategies, it is important to explore why these techniques are useful. She begins to understand that a second language is acquired in much the same way as a first; that a social setting offering encouragement and support without pressure allows the learner to begin producing oral language at his or her own rate. This "natural" approach, with constant support and modeling, allowed Sandy to spontaneously produce. Sandy's oral development occurred as she had opportunities to see vocabulary acted out.

Yet Meyer's commentary raises important questions that the teacher either ignores or is not aware of. What are they? How should they influence a teacher's plan for helping non-English speakers?

Closing the Discussion

Facilitators should provide time for group members to synthesize what they learned, and generate principles for teaching non-English speakers. They may also want to create a list of unresolved questions that need more attention.

Suggested Discussion Outline

1. What are the facts in the case?

    Probes:

    a. What actually happened?

    b. How did the teacher feel in each situation?

    c. What supports were noted in the second story that were not present in the first?

2. How would you compare the family situations of each student?

    Probes:

    a. Six-month stay versus immigration?

    b. Parental expectations? Why?

    c. Motivation to integrate into American society?

    d. Racial, gender differences? Implications?

3. How can you compare Magnus's, his brother's, and Sandy's developmental levels?

    Probes:

    a. What are the differences in developmental level?

    b. How do these differences affect their learning and socialization needs?

4. How would you describe the differences in the teacher's situation between the first story versus the second?

    Probes:

    a. New teacher versus veteran?

    b. District support?

    c. Perceptions of the students?

    d. Expertise and comfort with ESL strategies?

5. Let's look at the teacher's reflections on Magnus. What did she think were the causes of her problems?

   Probes:

   a. Were her hypotheses correct?

   b. Are there any hypotheses she may have over-looked?

   c. What disagreements, if any, do you have with her conclusions?

6. Now let's look at her reflections in the second situation. To what does she attribute her success?

   Probes:

   a. Were her hypotheses correct?

   b. Are there any questions she ignored or neglected to consider?

   c. What disagreements, if any, do you have with her conclusions?

7. What does Meyer's commentary have to add to this discussion?

   Probes:

   a. What questions does she raise?

   b. How does she compare the students in the first story and the second?

   c. How do her questions help you plan for/teach non-English speakers?

8. Describe some key issues in English-as-a-second-language acquisition.

   Probes:

   a. What is the natural approach?

   b. How would student grouping affect language acquisition?

   c. What classroom routines, activities, and structures are important?

9. Do you have any students in your classes who are non-English speakers? If yes, what do you do?

   Probes:

   a. What were your successes with these students?

   b. What were your disappointments?

   c How much support did you get from the district?

   d. What resources could you use to get more assistance?

10. What principles can you generate about dealing with non-English speaking students?

    Probes:

    a. What questions would you consider?

    b. What teaching methods would you use?

This case opens with the author describing herself: an overloaded, middle-school, bilingual teacher who has absorbed over 20 non-English-proficient (NEP) students since mid-year. She is frustrated with the tremendous responsibilities and demands placed upon her by the school's escalating cultural and linguistic diversity. Her overcrowded, under-supplied classroom is fairly bursting at the seams with youngsters unfamiliar with the North American educational setting. She is bothered by the students' hasty entrance and difficult adjustment.

Finally, in desperation, she joins forces with a creative writing teacher and creates a unique solution that involves bringing together fluent English-speaking students with non-English-speaking newcomers. The two teachers design a partners model that takes into account gender and culture. In addition, they design an information packet for the partners that includes basic knowledge like numbers, the alphabet, maps, addresses, and common conversational dialogues, plus cross-cultural games. The goals for their partnership program include nurturing friendships for the bilingual students, creating a sense of belonging in their new country, and providing culturally relevant material in English and Spanish.

The case traces the development of the student partnerships from apprehension and shyness to real interaction and learning. Most significant are the students' assessments of the project, which reflect their deep sense of responsibility and achievement. But the project also allows the teachers to identify areas that need improvement, such as materials development, grouping, flexibility, and native language instruction.

CONTEXT

This case presents a demographic microcosm of the cultural and linguistic challenges facing public schools. The overcrowded conditions, understaffing, and limited resources are typical of bilingual classrooms. Schools overwhelmed by expanding numbers of students must ask already-strained teachers to continue receiving these kids with no increase in materials or assistance. Students need extra help in other areas besides second language instruction. They hunger for information on U.S. culture, habits, customs, and behaviors. Some, like the Latin American students in this case, are making special adjustments. Because they have shifted from a calendar that begins in April to this country's September-June school cycle, they not only lose learning time, but also find themselves outsiders in classes where relationships have already been formed.

Many ESL teachers respond to these needs with innovation. In this case, the teachers turn to a buddy or partner system that provides newcomers with support from knowledgeable linguistic and cultural helpers. Because they are peers, these reassuring partners are better able than teachers to inspire more spontaneous language production. They also help reduce newcomers' anxiety about expressing themselves. At issue in the case is how a teacher creates these partnership structures with little or no institutional support, even as the immigrant population grows.

SEGMENTS OF THE DISCUSSION

What do we know about the teacher? This experienced ESL teacher feels the burden of responding to an overflow of students. Her reflections on previous teaching experiences in Latin America let us know that she is culturally knowledgeable about the world of the new immigrants she receives. It is apparent from the narrative that she feels singled out to handle the difficult load of so many newcomers. Is there any indication she resents this? Could the school administration handle student placement differently?

What do we know about the students? We know that these students, in general, have recently immigrated from Latin America. We can guess that if they come from Central America, particularly El Salvador, their circumstances are not ideal. Because of civil war, education is inconsistent. Violence and trauma mark everyday life. Youngsters who immigrate to the U.S. are often coping with wrenching separations, flashback memories, and a sense of guilt for leaving. For such students, the buddying and partnering project for writing and second language development answers multiple needs. It provides a built-in friendship, as well as a sense of cultural assurance that is particularly important for those who are shy and nervous. The pairing also allows youngsters to tell the stories of their homeland without embarrassment and might allow them to release some emotion in private with their buddy.

Second language issues. The teacher is quite candid about the deficits she sees in her creative model. She knows that second language acquisition must not exclude the need to continue native language instruction as a bridge, so that the academic momentum is not lost in the transition to a new culture and language. The use of native language could also have helped prepare youngsters for the academic tasks. We might examine other tactics for helping NEP students (see Kawazoe's commentary). Are there youngsters for whom this partnership model would not be successful?

CLOSING THE DISCUSSION

In this case, the teacher has been rather thorough in exploring her project and its flaws. While discussing this case, it might be helpful to compare this model with other ESL strategies that participants are aware of. The case might also be compared to "Then and Now: Insights Gained for Helping Children Learn English." Contrast the settings, grade level, and student needs, including those related to second language. How do the students' desires and needs differ as a result of their backgrounds? How are the teachers' strategies and methods different? Do the commentaries reflect these differences and similarities across cases?

SUGGESTED DISCUSSION OUTLINE

1. What characterizes this classroom setting?

   Probes:

   a. What are the goals?

   b. What do the students expect?

   c. What are the instructional approaches?

2. What do we know about this teacher?

   Probes:

   a. What were some of the attitudes held by the teacher regarding her job?

   b. What did she learn by the end of the project?

3. What were some of her strategies?

   Probes:

   a. How did the buddying help the students?

   b. What could have been done differently in the project?

   c. What about native language instruction?

4. Examine *One Student's Writing Process* in Kawazoe's commentary.

   Probes:

   a. What was the importance of the partner?

   b. How was this process similar to or different from the partner model described in the case?

5. What did the project accomplish?

   Probes:

   a. Did it meet the teacher's hopes?

   b. What could have been improved?

   c. What student needs were not met?

6. Compare the ESL strategies presented in previous cases (case 4: "Then and Now: Insights Gained for Helping Children Learn English") to this case.

   Probes:

   a. What were the similarities and differences?

   b. What are the advantages and disadvantages of each approach?

7. Can you generate any principles of instruction for integrating non-English speakers into a classroom?

This is possibly the casebook's most emotionally provocative narrative. On the surface, it focuses on a white, middle-class, "re-entry" teacher's difficulty with four disruptive black high school students and her search for constructive strategies to establish control in her classroom. At a deeper level, it deals with bias and naive ideas about the harsh realities of inner-city life. The teacher's honesty about her thoughts and feelings as she struggles to find solutions to her problems, coupled with the substantive commentaries from a black scholar, a veteran white teacher, and two new teachers of color, might kindle some passionate reactions to issues raised in the case.

Discussion of this case gives participants an opportunity to confront personal bias. As the teacher-author confronts her own prejudice and struggles to work through it, some participants may strongly identify with her dilemmas and reflect on their own. Others may be angry with the teacher's initial naiveté and bias towards blacks and may express their feelings with intensity. For these reasons, if this case is used in a seminar, it may be wise to delay discussing it until after group members have had an opportunity to establish trust with one another.

An intriguing sidetrack for this discussion is to compare this case to "Moments of Truth: Teaching *Pygmalion*." That case's author — also a middle-class, white veteran teacher — experienced similar insecurities and tensions while teaching *Pygmalion* to poor black high school students.

Though we don't usually recommend a particular structure, for this case we suggest that you conduct the discussion in two stages: the first before participants have read the commentaries, so they have a real chance to discover their personal responses; the second after they've read the commentaries and can discuss how they may have modified their critical judgments and analyses.

CONTEXT

This case takes place in a semi-rural, experimental magnet school near a large metropolitan area. The school is dominated by students from African-American and Latino working-class backgrounds, and has a reputation for campus disorder and low student achievement. One strategy for dealing with that situation was to increase teacher/student contact hours so teachers could develop personal relationships with their students.

The author portrays herself as an inexperienced, idealistic teacher who looked forward to broadening her "white, middle-class life" by helping minority students prepare for "successful and responsible American life." However, she admitted that she was unprepared to deal with some of the adolescents in her third-period class.

"The Gang of Four," all African-Americans from low socio-economic backgrounds, were this teacher's most difficult students. Veronica, a new mother, had to support her baby while attending school; Lee and Travis were fatherless and apparently adhered to little control at home; and Larry was strongly influenced by members of his church. Because of their situations, these students had to make adult-like life decisions that typical middle- and upper-class adolescents do not face. But unlike many students — particularly black males — in similar situations, these four did not drop out. They were "hanging in," despite the difficulties of staying in school.

SEGMENTS OF THE DISCUSSION

How you choose to explore this case depends on your purposes. One approach is to divide discussion into three parts, analyzing 1) the problems, 2) the roots of racial and socio-economic stereotypes, and 3) the teacher's intervention.

At the beginning of the discussion, ask "What is this case about?" Responses to this simple question will enable you to gauge where individuals stand on important issues. Some may say that it's a case of classroom control. Others may focus on the emotional elements and examine issues of bias, racism, and middle-class naiveté.

A cautionary note: Participants may label this teacher a racist, and attempt to prove it by quoting different parts of the narrative. This line of discussion has some merit, but is not an end in itself. At issue is the source and forms of racism, not the particular behaviors of this teacher or these students. Understanding the multiple interpretations of different parts of this narrative allows us to explore not only how the teacher could have handled her situation differently, but also how racist tendencies affect our own lives. (See commentaries, particularly Ramirez and Marchbanks.)

First day confrontation. At first reading, the "Gang of Four's" disruptions may seem to be simply a classroom management problem. The students, especially Veronica and her three friends, appear rude and undisciplined, and the teacher lacks the skills to take control. Upon closely analyzing what the teacher and students say, however, and viewing the situation from the students' perspective, the episode makes different sense. The teacher's idealistic speech can be construed as preachy and may have provoked students who were struggling to stay in school against terrible odds. All three commentators pick up on this and offer perceptive insights into why the students may have reacted as they did. In retrospect, the teacher also seems to feel that her initial actions were mistakes. (See the first part of her reflections at the end of the case.)

Baggage of stereotypes. Several kinds of stereotypes are evident in this case.

Sex-race stereotypes. In writing this case, the teacher-author took the opportunity to confront her preconceptions about the ghetto and particularly about African-American students. She wrote candid statements such as: "These students would have been a fearsome group in any color, but their blackness seemed at first to be a barrier," and then analyzed how this affected her

teaching. She also used descriptive language that reveals the depth of her feelings. For example, in depicting Veronica she wrote: "Stout, black, stuffed into a flame red dress, Veronica sauntered slowly, insolently past me. . . ."

It is possible that this kind of imagery reveals the teacher's unconscious fear of confronting blacks and consequently accounts for her inability to deal effectively with Veronica. In other words, a complex mix of racial and sexual perceptions may have influenced the teacher's way of responding to a real problem: an outspoken young woman in her classroom.

To understand this teacher's reaction to her confrontation with Veronica, we need to look at the prevalence in our society of sex-race caricatures or stereotyping. The "Jezebel" or "Sapphire" stereotype of African-American women is a highly charged portrayal of sexual aggression. Its relevance here is that it would "incorrectly equate [Veronica's] black skin and tight red dress to insolence." (See the Ramirez and Marchbanks commentary.) Sex-race stereotypes also came into play with other ethnic groups — for example, the "Fiery Señorita" image attributed to Latino women, or the Asian "Geisha" who is sexually pleasing, passive, and accommodating.

Socio-economic issues. A third stereotype that permeates this case relates to the teacher's perceptions of poverty — "the real enemy." As she explains, she tries to help students overcome the "poverty mentality," which consists of "apathy, laziness, and hopelessness." Thus, rather than judging the "Gang of Four" by their determination to get an education, the teacher draws on her preconceptions about them — ostensibly about their poverty, but this may also be a means by which the teacher allows herself to step back from the issue of race. (See the Ramirez and Marchbanks comments on the dangers of misinterpreting socio-economic issues.)

In essence, the teacher may simply be substituting one stereotype for another. She could have chosen to respect the students' commitment to school as a strong sign of their penchant for survival, endurance, and hope under difficult circumstances. She could have acknowledged their poverty and at-risk circumstances without simultaneously inferring negative inherent characteristics.

Perceptions of non-English speakers. Ramirez takes issue with the stereotype that non-English speaking Latino parents hinder their children's success in school because of their language deficit. Rather, she points out, Mexican-American families are often strong social units interested in helping their children excel. It is up to the schools to let these families know how best to support their children's education. (See the Ramirez-Marchbanks commentary.)

Color blindness. Ladson-Billings commends the teacher-author for being honest and open about her feelings towards blacks, because such topics are generally taboo. "Oh I don't see color. I just see children," is what teachers more commonly say about racial and ethnic differences among students. Yet, it appears that this author may have become "color blind" as she grew more comfortable with her black students. In the reflections section of the case, the teacher writes, ". . .I hardly notice that [people of color] are 'different,' because in fact they actually don't look different to me."

This topic of color blindness is complicated and emotionally charged. For the author, a person's blackness was initially alien and raised a host of stereotypes. As she acknowledged her own racism, she began to shed her negative feelings about people of color until she hardly noticed any differences. To her, this represented personal and professional growth. Yet, to persons of color like Marchbanks and Ramirez, the denial of differences is insulting.

Search for understanding and control. The teacher tried many strategies to gain control of her situation, but the "Gang of Four," especially Veronica, continued to challenge her authority. She sought help from others on the school staff, who were very supportive. She tried to develop a personal relationship with her students, an approach that is most important with minority students, as Ladson-Billings and Nelson-Barber point out in their commentaries. Her attempts led to deeper understanding and empathy for her students' circumstances, but did not significantly increase her classroom control. She still couldn't enjoy third period. In fact, she dreaded it.

During this section of the discussion, the facilitator might want to explore why the teacher had such disdain for this class and for these particular students. Why did she feel powerless to intervene appropriately? What was it about Veronica that was especially difficult? Was gender an issue? Veronica was a mother, with all of the adult responsibilities that role involves. Perhaps this teacher had difficulty relating to an adult woman in her classroom. Participants should examine why Veronica decided to speak individually to the teacher. What was she trying to communicate? (See Desser's commentary.)

The intervention. As the teacher reported, one day she realized that she was the only person who could solve her problem. "I needed to be not just a teacher, but a true leader in solving a group problem." Her strategy entailed not only telling the students her honest feelings, but also, and perhaps most important, listening to their suggestions. Apparently, her intervention worked; the students reported that they wanted her to take charge. The success of this strategy demonstrates the importance of reciprocity between teacher and students in developing consensus with one another.

One way to facilitate this part of the discussion is to ask the group to evaluate the teacher's intervention by giving her a letter grade, A-F. In determining a grade, participants should take into account the teacher's speech, the small group activities, the students' responses, and the indicators of success. They should also consider what other interventions the teacher might have used.

For comparison's sake, you may ask participants to read selected cases from *The Intern Teacher Casebook* (Shulman & Colbert (1988) available from the Far West Laboratory). All the cases are written by beginning teachers in a large metropolitan district who experience problems akin to those this author describes. Some used similar interventions but had different results. (See in particular "Painful Growth" in *The Intern Teacher Casebook*.)

CLOSING THE DISCUSSION

Since this discussion will probably raise more questions than it resolves, facilitators should take time as the session closes to debrief participants on what occurred and synthesize new insights. Many groups may want to revisit these issues in ensuing seminars.

SUGGESTED DISCUSSION OUTLINE

1. What is this case about?

2. Why did the first class get out of hand?

    Probes:

    a. What prompted the students' initial restlessness?

    b. Why do you think Veronica called the teacher a "fake preacher lady?"

    c. After the three black boys began dancing around the room, what message did the teacher communicate by proceeding to go about her business?

    d. What alternate opening speeches and first-day agendas might the teacher have considered?

    e. What are the risks and consequences for each approach?

3. What do we know about this teacher that would help explain some of her reactions?

    Probes:

    a. What do we know about her background?

    b. Why did she want to teach at this school?

    c. What was her mission for her students?

    d. What cues in the narrative help us understand her preconceptions about African-American students and their family circumstances (perceptions toward race, socio-economic causes, color)?

4. What might provoke the "Gang of Four" to respond in the manner described?

    Probes:

    a. What do we know about their background?

    b. What do they gain from continually challenging the teacher's control?

    c. How do they perceive this teacher? Why?

    d. How do the other students feel about the "Gang of Four"?

5. How can we make sense out of the troubled relationship between Veronica and the teacher?

    Probes:

    a. Are there any gender issues involved?

    b. What difference might it make that Veronica is a mother?

c. Why did Veronica write the teacher a note on the first day of class?

d. Why is Veronica hostile toward the teacher?

e. Why do you think the teacher is particularly uncomfortable with Veronica?

6. On reflecting back on this experience, the teacher is pleased that she no longer notices differences in people's color. What is implied in this statement?

Probes:

a. From the teacher's perspective?

b. From the perspective of persons of color?

7. What might explain the source of racial and socio-economic stereotypes?

Probes:

a. Middle-class background?

b. Lack of experience with other racial groups and poverty?

c. Disposition to refrain from talking about racism in public?

8. Now let's turn to the teacher's intervention. What turned the tide in this classroom?

Probes:

a. What are some of the positive approaches that the teacher tried (e.g., seeking outside resources)?

b. What are the positive consequences of establishing personal relationships? Are there any risks involved?

c. What are some of the organizational support systems for pursuing these goals?

9. How would you evaluate the teacher's candid speech and cooperative group activity? Support your answer.

Probes:

a. What might have happened if the teacher had not solicited student opinions?

b. How did this intervention affect the teacher's and students' subsequent thoughts and feelings for this class?

c. How did this change affect the teacher's capacity to provide meaningful instruction to this class?

10. What new insights did you gain from this case discussion?

Case 7

Drained by One Troubled Child: Did I Help?

The dilemmas in this poignant case are all too common in inner-city settings. The main character, Eric, is an African-American third-grade boy who was taken from his mother's abusive home and sent to live with his caring grandmother. Because of a series of events described in the case, he travels alone across the city to school. After Christmas, his moderately disruptive behavior becomes dramatically worse; he acts hostile, sometimes violent, toward the teacher and other students, refuses to do work, and often sabotages instruction. After several unsuccessful attempts by the teacher, principal, counselor, social worker, and school site team to mediate his behavior, Eric is referred to a class for emotionally disturbed children at another school.

The story is told by a white veteran teacher who has taught at the school for 13 years and believes she understands and appreciates the local "way of life." Her struggles with Eric, she feels, made that year her most difficult in 30 years of teaching. This teacher goes to unusual lengths to find ways to help Eric. She tries many of the conventional pedagogical practices and convenes extensive meetings with the grandmother and all appropriate school personnel. Yet no one is really able to help her cope with Eric in her classroom.

Feelings of frustration, sadness, and guilt permeate this teacher's story. She can't seem to break through to the child, the system fails to provide adequate classroom assistance, she worries that she didn't do enough for Eric, and she feels she neglected to meet the needs of the 29 other children in her classroom.

The commentators — a black scholar, a black staff developer, and a white teacher — raise issues from several perspectives. The first two commentators affirm that this teacher appeared to genuinely care about the child, but raise questions about some of the methods she used to help. They also point out that the majority of special education students in many districts are black males and ask, "Is this the best place for our children?" The third commentator, who has observed the teacher-

author, is angry and saddened that this outstanding teacher, who has exhausted all of the conventional strategies that would have helped most students and feels guilty about not doing enough.

Without more support, she questions whether it is realistic for teachers to feel they are responsible for making a critical difference in every student's life.

It may be useful to compare this teacher-author's approach to that of the teacher in Case 8: "Darius: I Hope He Makes It!" Both cases deal with black youngsters who are hurting. But the teachers' tactics and strategies for working with these boys are quite different.

CONTEXT

The school is located in a predominantly African-American neighborhood and also serves students who are bused in from other areas. It appears to have an active support system for needy children — counselors, social workers, and school site teams — yet is less able to really help the teachers who work with those children.

SEGMENTS OF THE DISCUSSION

The first part of the discussion should focus on the facts of the case and the participants' diagnosis of the problems. Then ask: How else could the problem be framed? From Eric's perspective? From the mother or grandmother's perspective? From the resource people's perspective?

What do we know about Eric? Eric is one of the growing number of children in inner cities who are separated from their parents because of substance abuse and incarceration and sent to live with their grandparents or some other caregiver. We know that Eric is a needy child. He wishes he were in fourth grade with his peers, but he does not know how to convey this desire to school authorities. We can surmise that he wants to be with his mother; yet when she is able to visit him, his behavior is less controlled in school. He demonstrates that he much prefers to stay in this teacher's class than to return home for half-days. When under stress, however, he does not (perhaps cannot) adapt to the expected norm of student behavior; he refuses to do work, harasses other children, disrupts instruction, and is occasionally violent with the teacher and other students. We know nothing specific about his mother or about the kind of abuse Eric experienced in her household. It does appear, however, that Eric's grandmother is a caring person; she has spent a great deal of time with school personnel trying to be helpful.

Youngsters like Eric are generally viewed by teachers as "problems" because of the disruptions they create in class and their volatile behavior on the playground. Indeed, these children often command much extra attention from teachers, administrators, and other resource personnel. In our day-to-day lives as teachers, however, we often forget how much some children must endure to come to school. Books like Samuel Freedman's *Small Victories* and Alex Katlowitz's *There Are No Children Here* are excellent reminders of the harsh surroundings that many children, particularly black youngsters who live in project housing, must tolerate daily. After reading these books, people with no first-hand knowledge of these living conditions may temper their view of "problem students" with admiration for these youngsters staying in school at all.

What do we know about the teacher? This white veteran teacher has taught for 30 years, 13 of them in the same school building. She says she has developed a sound relationship with the community and feels she understands and appreciates "their way of life." From her narrative, it appears that she is a dedicated teacher who works hard to provide a solid learning environment for all of her students. When that mission is compromised, however, like it was in this case, she feels frustrated and guilty. Zolli's commentary offers confirming evidence of her skills as a teacher. We learn that her

classroom is "interactive, visually and academically stimulating, and personalized."

What's clear is the enormous challenge that Eric presented to this teacher. She sees him as responsible for her most difficult year of teaching. What were some of her interventions for helping him? Were any successful? How did district specialists respond to her classroom problems?

How can teachers help kids like Eric? After clarifying techniques the teacher actually tried with Eric, it is critical to examine what alternative approaches she could have considered. Ladson-Billings' and Haysbert's commentaries help provide some insights and specific ideas. They emphasize the importance of establishing a personal relationship with a "hurting child" and shed light on the special needs of African-American students (especially males).

One of the many unsuccessful approaches the teacher used was to develop contracts about finishing his school work. Perhaps these could have been tied to Eric's need for some internal discipline over his violent behavior. For example, the teacher might have created specific incremental agreements that could be linked to what Eric wanted most: being promoted to fourth grade. In doing so, it's important to start with short intervals, such as daily evaluations, then work up to longer time periods to ensure the possibility of success. Interventions like this may have life-long benefits.

After discussing other strategies the teacher could have used with Eric, ask participants to share their own experiences. How can a teacher establish a personal relationship with her students? Is race an issue in this? Are some strategies particularly helpful with certain ethnic groups? What are the risks and consequences of each? How would you describe the personal relationship between the teacher and Eric?

A cautionary note: Many teachers — especially novices — might argue that teachers' hands are tied unless they have the full support of their students' families. They blame the victim — in this case Eric — for his behavior in school and assume that nothing can be done because his personal problems are so acute. Some may suggest that teachers simply have to "cut their losses" and never question whether different strategies might have made a difference.

Facilitators should note that lengthy discussions on topics like these may be very active and cathartic, but they can easily disintegrate into complaint sessions where no real learning occurs. Our experience suggests that the facilitator needs to direct the discussion away from whether to blame the teacher or the victim and toward exploring constructive, less conventional approaches that appear to work with African-American youngsters. Otherwise, time may run out before alternative approaches are discussed.

Where can teachers get help? One of the biggest issues for teachers who have problems with individual students is figuring out how and where to get help. The teacher in this case sought guidance from outside experts, but the topic of conversation was always focused on what was best for Eric, not on specific alternative approaches for the teacher. Moreover, the social service team appeared reluctant to disclose confidential family information. Where can/should teachers look for help?

One possibility is from other teachers who have similar problems. School-site case conferences can be established, during which individual teachers present specific dilemmas, brainstorm alternate solutions with colleagues, and ultimately learn from one another. Another possibility is to read and discuss relevant articles in groups. Several such articles, dealing specifically with the needs of African-American children like Eric, are listed in the casebook's bibliography.

Retention. In the epilogue to this case, the teacher-author seriously questions the school's retention policy.

This may be a topic worth pursuing in the case discussion. Extensive research shows that for most students retention not only doesn't help, but is counterproductive. As noted in *It's Elementary,* California's blueprint for elementary education, retained children have lower self-esteem and poorer attitudes toward school than matched classmates who were promoted. But most important, they do less well academically after the experience. Research also shows that students most likely to repeat a grade are those whose parents have marginal educations and incomes. And a disproportionately high number are African-Americans, Latinos, or recent immigrants.

Teachers may want to discuss their own experiences with retention policies. They may want to brainstorm ways of giving students special supports that would allow them to move to the next grade.

What's realistic? The Zolli commentary questions the tendency for successful teachers to feel that they should be able to handle all situations despite the obstacles. As a result, they "trip over their own success" and can end up with immeasurable frustration and guilt over their failures. How much should teachers expect of themselves? Is it realistic to expect to make a difference in all students' lives? Is it acceptable to let some students go?

CLOSING THE DISCUSSION

The discussion should end with the more general questions that provoke continued deliberation outside of class. What is the best way to educate children with special needs? Do they belong in classes for the emotionally disturbed? Is special education the answer? What are the implications of the fact that, in many districts, the majority of children in special education are African-American males?

SUGGESTED DISCUSSION OUTLINE

1. What are the facts/key elements in this case?

2. What is your analysis of the problem?

   Probes:

   a. What conclusions can you draw from the description?

   b. What evidence do you have to support your conclusions?

   c. How would the case have differed if the teacher had not hurt herself controlling Eric in the fight?

   d. What would have happened if the teacher had kept Eric seated near her even after his disruptive behavior?

   e. What would have happened if Eric had not been put on a restricted, half-day schedule?

3. How else can the problem be framed?

   Probes:

   a. From Eric's perspective?

   b. From the mother/grandmother's perspective?

   c. From the principal's and resource personnel's perspective?

   d. From the other students' perspective?

4. What do we know about Eric?

   Probes:

   a. Family situation?

   b. Hypotheses for change in behavior after the Christmas holidays?

   c. How do we know that Eric wants to stay in this classroom?

5. What classroom techniques and external resources did the teacher use to mediate Eric's behavior?

   Probes:

   a. What were the pros and cons of her tactics?

   b. What were their effects on Eric? On the rest of the students?

6. What alternate strategies could she have considered?

   Probes:

   a. Are there any that may be more sensitive to the needs of "hurting children" — particularly black males? (Refer to Ladson-Billings and Haysbert commentaries.)

   b. What are the risks and consequences associated with each strategy?

   c. How are this teacher's tactics different from those of the teacher who wrote Case 8: "Darius: I Hope He Makes It"?

7. Do you think race was a factor in this case?

   Probe:

   a. How might this case be different if Eric were white?

8. In the teacher's epilogue, she re-evaluates both the district's decision to retain Eric and the principle of retention in general. What do you think about retaining students?

a. Do you think Eric should have been retained?
    Would his situation have been different had he
    not repeated a grade? How? Why?

b. What are the advantages and disadvantages of
    retaining students?

c. What are the risks and consequences?

9. When the specialists fail to provide constructive
    classroom assistance with children, how can teach-
    ers get help from one another?

    Probes:

    a. What about case conferences?

    b. What about discussion groups on relevant
        articles?

10. How realistic is the expectation of many successful
    teachers that, despite all obstacles, they should be
    able to handle any situation?

    Probes:

    a. Is it realistic to believe that a teacher can reach
        all students?

    b. Is it acceptable to let some students go?

    c. What are the implications of each decision?

    d. What do you think of the belief that teachers
        must "cut their losses"?

11. What is the best educational setting for youngsters
    like Eric?

a. Is special education the answer?

b. What are the implications of the fact that the
    majority of students in special education are
    black males?

This case, a possible companion to the previous narrative, "Drained By One Troubled Child," describes a teacher's struggle to cope with and help Darius, a nine-year-old black child who came to her classroom with a history of low achievement and violence. Unlike Eric's teacher, who never seemed to make headway with Eric no matter what tactics she used, this teacher's approaches appeared to make a difference in Darius's classroom work and, marginally, in his behavior with other students. Unfortunately, this progress was dramatically reversed when the administrators suspended Darius for violent behavior on the playground. Though there were minor gains during the two months after the suspension, Darius never returned to his previous "good" behavior.

This narrative is one of the few in this casebook that illustrates apparently effective ways of dealing with troubled black male youngsters. What were these successful approaches? How do they differ from the tactics that Eric's teacher tried? Why did Darius appear to respond better to this teacher than to those of previous years? How did the teacher-author regard Darius? What did she have going for her? The commentary by Gloria Ladson-Billings, a black scholar who has studied why some teachers are more successful with black children than others, provides insight into many of these questions. Peg Foley Reynolds provides a veteran teacher's perspective in her commentary.

CONTEXT

This case takes place in an inner-city school, one targeted for special school funding because of its high proportion of low-achieving, at-risk students. Darius's past two years at school had been marred by his restriction to a half-day schedule because of his violent behavior with other students.[1] The reported comments indicate that his third and fourth grade teachers at best merely tolerated

---

[1] A restricted half-day schedule was also used for Eric, in the previous case.

him. They clearly didn't demand much work. Because he was a "good reader," the fourth grade teacher had put him in reading groups every morning "until he got bored." When disruptive, he went to the principal's office to wait for dismissal at lunch.

Like Eric, Darius is a black male youngster whose home life is marked by considerable trauma. Though the case provides little information about his family background or the origin of his problems, we discover that Darius's mother was murdered a month after the case was written. Because of his repeated violent behavior with other children at school, we can assume he experienced violence at home.

SEGMENTS OF THE DISCUSSION

The first part of the discussion should focus on what actually happened in the case and the participants' diagnosis of the problems. When did the teacher discover that she would get Darius in her classroom? What did the teacher do? What happened?

What do we know about the teacher? This veteran teacher has a racially mixed background — part white, part Native American, and raised in a Latino culture — and has an excellent reputation for her success with inner-city, at-risk children. Her skillful use of strategies such as conflict resolution and active listening help children cope with their problems by talking about them rather than acting out by abusing their classmates or other people around them. She also directs the school's Conflict Managers Program which trains individual children to use conflict resolution skills with their peers on the schoolyard.

What is clear from reading her narrative is that, unlike many teachers, she was able to look beyond "Darius, the classroom problem," to "Darius, the individual." She describes him as a troubled child who is "particularly bright and insightful." Though initially annoyed to discover that she would have yet another "problem" in her classroom the following year, the teacher began to plan immediately for Darius's arrival. She talked to former teachers, looked through his academic records, and devised schemes to counter some of the apparently low-level educational experiences he had endured in the third and fourth grades. Discussion participants may want to talk about how they might plan for integrating "problem" students into their own classrooms.

Motivational strategies. One of the most important goals of this case discussion is to examine the tactics this teacher used to motivate Darius to cooperate in her classroom. Developing contracts, nurturing a personal relationship, and initiating physical contact such as hugging and flipping are some of the techniques that she mentioned in the case.

Ladson-Billings' commentary provides wonderful insights into why Darius responded to her. She discusses the importance of cultivating a personal relationship with black, at-risk youngsters like Darius, and examines other aspects of effectively working with African-American youngsters. During the discussion, participants should share strategies that they have tried with at-risk children — especially troubled black male youngsters — and offer explanations about why the approaches worked or didn't.

Raising expectations. According to the research literature, teachers commonly lower their expectations of what at-risk children can learn. When this happens, bright students often come to believe that they are slow learners and begin to act like it. Researchers, like Rhona Weinstein from the University of California-Berkeley and Henry Levin from Stanford University, point out how much harm can result. They urge teachers instead to raise their expectations of what children-at-risk can accomplish and then provide support to help them meet these expectations.

One now-famous teacher who epitomized this philosophy is Jaime Escalante, whose work with remedial math students led to their passing the Advanced Placement mathematics test. Escalante was a masterful teacher. He provided excellent instruction, making sure to relate key math concepts to his students' life experiences. He also encouraged students to work hard and persuaded them to believe that they could be successful.

The suspension. Darius's progress abruptly halted after he was suspended: he returned to his hostile, argumentative behavior. Analysis should focus on how the teacher handled the situation, and why Darius was so hostile. Ladson-Billings's examination of Darius's actions should be very helpful in this analysis.

Facilitators should be cautioned that discussion of the suspension could easily deteriorate into a bull session about what happens when principals are uncooperative. Though talking about this topic can be relevant and cathartic, discussion should advance beyond mere complaints. Any analysis of this case should also deal with the administrators' perspective. For example, what are the ramifications of Darius's hostile behavior toward other students? To whom are administrators accountable? To teachers? To students? To parents? Are there any situations where it may be appropriate to override the wishes of faculty?

Closing the Discussion

As discussion draws to a close, facilitators should make sure the group understands that the teacher's personal relationship with Darius was important to his growth. That special relationship, however, also contributed to his anger when he felt betrayed by the teacher.

Suggested Discussion Outline

1. What actually happened in this case?

2. What do we know about the teacher?

Probes:

   a. Background and ethnicity?

   b. Reputation?

3. What approaches did she use to deal with conflict?

Probes:

   a. Active listening?

   b. Conflict resolution?

   c. Other?

4. What were the variety of tactics that she used with Darius when he came into her classroom?

Probes:

   a. Cultivate a personal relationship?

   b. Physical contact (e.g., hugs, flipping)?

   c. Contracts?

   d. Raise expectations?

5. What other approaches could this teacher have used?

Probe:

   a. What are the risks and consequences of each approach?

6. Compare this teacher's tactics to those of Eric's teacher in Case 7: "Drained By One Troubled Child: Did I Help?")

Probes:

   a. How are they similar?

   b. How are they different?

   c. What can we learn from each approach?

7. What do we know about Darius?

Probes:

   a. Family background?

   b. Experience with former teachers?

   c. Behavior with peers?

   d. How can we account for his behavior in class and on the playground?

8. Why did Darius appear to respond to this teacher more positively than his previous teachers?

9. Now let's turn to the suspension. What were the consequences for Darius?

Probes:

   a. Why was Darius hostile to his teacher? To other students?

   b. Based on his former experiences with teachers, why should he trust any teacher?

   c. Do you think that the suspension influenced the way other students regarded Darius? Why?

10. How did the teacher handle the situation?

Probes:

a. Immediately after the suspension?

b. During the episode in class two weeks later?

c. What other approaches could she have used?

d. What were the repercussions of the situation?

e. What is the worst possible scenario? What is the best scenario?

11. Now look at this case from the administrators' perspective. How would they have framed the problems?

Probes:

a. To whom are administrators accountable (e.g., faculty, students, parents)?

b. What are the repercussions of administrators failing to be responsible for each of the above groups?

c. Are there any situations where it may be appropriate to override the wishes of faculty?

12. Describe some of the students in your class who cause problems. What approaches have you used that have been effective? Which ones have been ineffective?

Probes:

a. Have you received any support with these students? If yes, what kind?

b. Given this case discussion, can you think of any tactics to use with these students that you had not previously considered?

13. Are there any principles that you can generate from this and other cases on teaching troubled youngsters, particularly black males?

This Filipino/Chicano resource teacher, who considered himself outstanding not only as a teacher but as a role model for Latino students, substituted for the regular Spanish teacher on sick leave for a number of weeks. He was taken aback by the difficulty he had with a group of 12 fifth-grade Latino students, who were pulled out of their regular class for an hour each day to get native language instruction. The students were hostile and disruptive, tried to sabotage assigned tasks, and refused to speak Spanish. The teacher expected the students to resist talking in their native language. What he found unusual was the intensity of their resistance.

On the surface, this case is about a teacher who has problems with classroom management. When we dig deeper, however, and examine the situation from a variety of perspectives — political, sociological, psychological and pedagogical — we can begin to understand the cause of the students' disruptive behavior.

Commentator Richard Piper, who has studied bilingual programs for several years, not only reacts to the case, but sets the stage for discussions on bilingual education. Amado Padilla offers the perspective of the educational psychologist in his commentary. And Lori Murakami and Anna Yamaguchi, bilingual teachers themselves, add a practical viewpoint to the discussion.

CONTEXT

The case takes place in a school where tensions exist between two minority cultural communities, Chinese and Latino. At issue is cultural conflict among minority groups, an increasingly common theme in large urban areas where the white population — long the majority group — is now decreasing.

This school is trying to comply with two political directives. The first is the state's bilingual mandate, which requires the district to provide native language instruction for all students designated as Limited-English Proficient (LEP). The second is the district's

Consent Decree, designed to achieve ethnic integration and equal educational opportunity for all students. At times, schools find it difficult to balance political compliance with efforts to achieve educational excellence for all students.

This school, located in a traditionally Asian neighborhood, has resisted integration. It now houses two separate bilingual programs: Chinese bilingual classes whose students live in the neighborhood, and Spanish bilingual classes, whose Latino students are bused in from other parts of the city. According to state and district policy, bilingual classes must contain a small proportion of fluent-English-proficient speakers (FEPs) who can act as model English speakers for the rest of the class. Apparently, the native Spanish-speaking students described in this case were placed in the Chinese bilingual class because of their fluency in English.

It should be noted that the logistics in this case are quite atypical, even for this district. When the bilingual mandate was originally conceived, it was assumed that native English speakers would be used as role models for LEP students. However, in many urban schools there simply are not enough native English speakers to go around. Moreover, there are often not enough credentialed bilingual teachers to meet student demand. In this case, all of the bilingual and English Language Development classes[2] were filled, so these students were placed in a Chinese bilingual class that was taught primarily in English.

SEGMENTS OF THE DISCUSSION

It may be useful to begin this session with a discussion of the case's political and sociological context — in particular, the purposes and rationales for bilingual programs and integration policies. Piper's and Padilla's commen-

---

[2] English Language Development classes (ELDs) are transition classes from bilingual to mainstream English classes.

taries can help. Piper provides informative background on both bilingual education and the challenges of teaching LEP students. Padilla questions the intent of the Consent Decree, especially when students are "used" to achieve ethnic balance in a particular school.

Then discuss what actually happened in the narrative. What did the teacher plan for his pull-out group? How did the students respond? How did the teacher accommodate his students' unanticipated reactions?

What do we know about the teacher? This Filipino/Chicano veteran teacher, who reports that he is deeply committed to bilingual education throughout the elementary years, considers himself a role model for Chicano students. Trained in conflict resolution, he feels equipped to handle a multitude of problems and to linguistically and personally validate students' concerns. Though Padilla questions some of the teacher's tactics (see below), the teacher feels he is well liked by his students and knows how to present instruction suitable to their learning styles. Thus, he is genuinely shocked at the students' negative reactions.

Instructional plans and methods. Though the teacher states that he had planned to present an innovative cultural and literature-based Spanish program, he actually used games, dittos, and cutting and pasting exercises to teach Spanish in his first few classes. The teacher admits that these "unchallenging activities" made for a "watered-down curriculum," but he felt the need to keep the students busy and thought these activities would do that. Later on he tries other conventional approaches — a basal reader and short stories written in Spanish — to which the students seem to respond more favorably.

When the teacher saw how negatively the students reacted to his lessons, he hypothesized that their problems were due to low self-esteem. So he tried to improve their self-images by: 1) personally validating them in culturally familiar ways with "sincere" physical contact

(e.g., hugs) and terms of endearment; 2) having 20-minute individual counseling sessions (during the regular program); 3) sending validation letters to students on official stationery; and 4) calling them at home.

What other hypotheses could account for the students' hostile behavior? How appropriate were these methods? Participants should examine the appropriateness of all of the teacher's strategies. From the case information above, however, this may be hard to do. We don't know, for example, the goals and purposes for this pull-out program. Since "maintenance" of native languages is not part of the district's goals for bilingual education, perhaps the school designated one hour of native language instruction as an enrichment activity. Yet even if this were the case, what were students supposed to learn in this program? If this teacher had communicated with the regular teacher to establish common purposes and continuity of instruction, perhaps he could have planned more appropriate instructional units. At the very least, he would have been better able to assess the students' reactions.

How developmentally appropriate were the teacher's activities? The initial games and cut-and-paste activities appear to be more appropriate for primary students than fifth graders. Possibly the youngsters were simply turned off. Murakami and Yamaguchi suggest more creative projects such as "plays, skits, music, and dance integrated with literature, science, and math activities — all incorporating the Spanish language." What are other alternatives?

It appears that the teacher invested more energy in out-of-class efforts to raise students' self-esteem than in planning meaningful instruction. From his description, these activities had positive results. The students were more responsive in his class, and their regular teacher said that some had turned in more work. How appropriate were the teacher's methods? What are the advantages and disadvantages of these personal investments? What are the risks and consequences of these activities?

Padilla questions the case writer's use of "terms of endearment" with his students. These are terms usually saved for communicating with family members, not with strangers. It is especially inappropriate for men to use such terms with older children. What are some other ways the teacher could have shown respect and affection for his students?

Sociological/psychological/political influences. Other factors may explain the students' dislike of this pull-out bilingual program. Some educators, like Padilla, argue that students may feel like second-class citizens when they are bused to another neighborhood, especially when "this is done simply to achieve some sort of arbitrary court-mandated ethnic balance." This argument may be particularly salient for Latinos who are bused into a Chinese-American neighborhood.

Other commentators, like Nelson-Barber and Mesa-Bains, maintain that different cultural styles of interaction might cause tension between students and teachers. The case writer also notes possible ethnic differences in interactional behaviors between Latinos and Chinese-Americans. Latino students often thrive in environments where nurturing teachers encourage lots of spontaneity and activity. Chinese-Americans, on the other hand, are generally rewarded for disciplined and reserved behavior. The Latino students in this case may have been uncomfortable in a classroom where expectations for appropriate behavior were vastly different from their own culturally accepted norms. Conversely, the teacher may have perceived the Latino students' behavior as disrespectful and antagonistic, and may have displayed favoritism toward students who acted in more familiar ways.

What about the students' general resistance to speak in their native language? Piper notes that this is not uncommon, since youngsters generally do not want to appear different in the eyes of their peers.

Did the students in this case suffer from low self-esteem? Padilla questions this assessment, which this teacher appears to apply to all low-achieving minority students. Instead of expending so much energy trying to build his students' self-esteem through cultural affirmation, perhaps the teacher should have emphasized their sense of powerlessness and exclusion from the Chinese-dominated classroom.

CLOSING THE DISCUSSION

One way to close this session is to discuss how realistic the teacher's aspirations were about what he could accomplish during his five weeks with these students. (Padilla addresses this problem at the end of his commentary.) Another tactic is to encourage participants to share their own experiences with bilingual pull-out programs and integration policies. What do they think are the advantages and disadvantages of these programs? How would these students answer that question? What new insights did this case discussion stimulate? Can they generate any principles from this discussion?

SUGGESTED DISCUSSION OUTLINE

As stated earlier, it may be useful to begin this session by discussing the purposes and rationales for bilingual programs and integration policies. This background knowledge is essential for understanding some of the key elements described in the narrative. (See Padilla's and Piper's commentaries.)

1. What actually happened?

2. Why did "a trip to hell" happen? Why did the teacher experience so many problems with his pull-out Spanish program?

3. What do we know about the teacher?

Probes:

a. What was the teacher's background?

b. How qualified was he to teach this class?

c. What did he want to accomplish?

4. What do we know about the Latino students in this class?

Probes:

a. What were their backgrounds? New immigrants? Second generation? Do we know?

b. Why do they go to a special Spanish class?

c. How do you think that the students (both Latino and Chinese-American) perceive the pull-out program?

d. What do you think about the situation?

5. What do we know about the context of this case?

Probes:

a. Why were these Spanish bilingual fifth grade students placed in this Chinese bilingual class?

b. Why were Latino students bused to this Asian school?

c. How does the state's bilingual mandate affect this situation?

d. What are some of the differences and similarities in values between the Chinese and Latino communities?

6. Let's look at the teacher's instructional plans for the class.

Probes:

a. What did the teacher hope to accomplish in his class?

b. What specific strategies did he use?

c. How did he adjust his instructional strategies when he saw how strongly the students resisted?

7. How appropriate were those strategies?

Probes:

a. What other strategies could the teacher have tried?

b. What are the risks and consequences for each one?

8. Why do you think the students were so disruptive in the first class and during ensuing classes?

Probes:

a. Inappropriate instruction?

b. Change of teacher?

c. Reaction to possible pent-up emotions during regular class?

d. Why did they refuse to speak Spanish?

9. Now let's look at the teacher's interventions to provide effective support and raise students' self-esteem.

Probes:

a. What specific strategies did he use?

b. What were the consequences of these tactics?

c. How appropriate were these interventions?

d. Can you think of other interventions for these kids?

e. Do you think that these kids suffered from low esteem?

f. How appropriate is the use of "terms of endearment" with students?

10. The teacher was pleased with some of the consequences of his interventions. What were some of these changes in behavior?

Probes:

a. How much can we attribute to the teacher's interventions?

b. How much change is feasible to expect in such a short time?

11. What do you think about the advantages and disadvantages of bilingual pull-out programs?

Probes:

a. What effect do these programs have on the students in the program? On the other students? On the regular classroom teacher?

b. How do/can these programs help students?

c. How do/can they harm students?

d. Can you think of ways to improve the programs?

12. Based on this discussion and your experience, what principles can we generate about the issues discussed in this case? How do they relate to those generated in previous discussions? Have you had to adapt any existing principles because of new knowledge and insights?

From "Outsider" to Active Learner: Struggles in a Newcomer School

In an all-Latino newcomer school receiving mainly new immigrants to a rural area, teachers struggle to provide a balance of academic skills, cultural support, and knowledge of U.S. schooling and society. This story gives us insight into the student's experience in such a school. The teacher reflects on her second year of teaching, the year when a troublesome third grader, Mario, entered her class.

Early on, this teacher is clearly trying to head off problems with Mario when she tells the class of her emphasis on goals, rules, and routines. As a Latina herself from an immigrant working class background, this teacher sets such rules with an awareness of the cultural adjustment her students are making. While attempting to support Latino values of respect for authority, she also steers them away from absolute obedience and toward a more interdependent autonomy.

Despite this outlook, she reacts with frustration and anger when Mario seems unable to be responsible about academic work. After she explodes at him and insists that his mother come see her, she discovers that behind his tough facade he is a vulnerable child with a difficult family life. Their emotional exchange leads to a deeper personal relationship. Ultimately, his mother does come, and the alliance of school and home helps Mario blossom. The case ends on a positive note: Mario has new confidence in his abilities and is growing academically, and the teacher feels that her beliefs about teaching and learning have been validated.

CONTEXT

The newcomer school setting allows us to gain some understanding of the complexity of the immigrant situation, the heterogeneity of a shared culture, and the importance of native language development, as well as ESL, in preparing youngsters for regular classrooms. This case lets us examine the difficulties of school-home connections even when teacher and family share the same language and culture.

The immigrant situation is filled with trauma and change. Entering a new school setting, as well as a society with different language and social demands, puts great pressure on students. Often, they are called upon to help adult family members navigate an unfamiliar language and culture. Though we don't know the specifics of Mario's family problems, family tension and sometimes violence are not unusual among immigrants who are socially and economically displaced, possibly suffering traumatic loss, and also seeking employment. One way these problems manifest is student apathy.

The teacher in this case gives us rich information on her instructional and curricular strategies and on the role of native language instruction. Her ability to set clear, predictable outcomes, goals, and expectations is especially important for newcomers who may be completely redefining their understandings of "learner" and "teacher." Knowing what behaviors are expected makes students feel safe. It alleviates the newcomers' apprehension and anxiety. Pringle's commentary sheds light on how newcomer schools are structured to prepare students for the larger society.

SEGMENTS OF THE DISCUSSION

Discussion of the newcomer setting, characteristics, and goals will help set the stage for looking at the relationship between Mario and his teacher. What do we know about the newcomer school? What are the goals of this transitional setting? What are the instructional and curricular characteristics of this kind of school? How is it different from a regular school setting?

What do we know about the teacher? This Chicana teacher was born into an immigrant family from Mexico. Her early years were marked by struggle. Influenced in her early adulthood by the civil rights movement for Chicanos — "El Movimiento" — her beliefs stem from a deep commitment to cultural self-determination. Her own bi-cultural experience inspires her to help the students adjust their more traditional obedience to authority to a more open and expressive view of their own autonomy. Since she had been teaching only two years at the time of this episode, we know that Mario presented one of her first significant challenges. We also know that she sees native language instruction and a culturally supportive curriculum as essential to the newcomer program.

Early strategies. The teacher's emphasis on clear rules and routines creates a comforting predictability for immigrant youngsters, who are in the midst of much change in their lives. Mario, however, had an emotional need for personal contact. The teacher's "get tough" stance may have overwhelmed him. Until her conflict with Mario, she may have overlooked the importance of a balance in newcomer schools between focusing on classroom behaviors and building links to family and home life.

The crisis and intervention. In confronting Mario about his failure to produce homework and, subsequently, to bring in his mother, the teacher discovers this child's deeper emotional life. She is touched and responds with empathy. In Latino cultures, where personal connections are highly valued, this student-teacher catharsis serves as the beginning of a new relationship.

The teacher's display of real concern for Mario introduces an element often uncomfortable to mainstream teaching — a teacher's personal involvement with his or her students. In the newcomer setting, where the teacher's role is to help the family bridge the differences between home culture and the new culture, such personal connection is a necessity. Nelson-Barber's commentary helps us understand the value many Latino groups place on mutual respect, loving care, and student determination — *respeto*, *cariño*, and *ganas*.

The outcome. The way in which both Mario and his family respond to the teacher's new personal relation-ship with them indicates its level of importance. The teacher's heartfelt outreach is not a substitute for good classroom management or instruction, but rather an extension of a wholistic approach to teaching and learning. Discussing the teacher's three major beliefs, in light of her strategies and interventions, would further the overall understanding of the case.

SUGGESTED DISCUSSION OUTLINE

1. What characterizes the newcomer school setting?

   Probes:

   a. What are the goals? (See Pringle's commentary.)

   b. What are the curricular and instructional approaches?

   c. What about home-school contact?

2. What do we know about this teacher?

   Probes:

   a. What insights from her self-description strike you?

   b. What insights from the Nelson-Barber commentary are relevant?

   c. What were some of the cultural issues between the student and teacher?

   d. How do the concepts *respeto*, *cariño*, and *ganas* (from Torres-Guzman in the Nelson-Barber commentary) apply in this case?

3. What were her early strategies?

Probes:

a. What was her rationale for the rules and routines emphasis?

b. What were the pros and cons of the "get tough" approach with Mario?

c. What was the importance of her cultural curriculum approach?

d. What else could she have done to facilitate Mario's entrance into the class?

4. What were the key issues between teacher and student during the crisis?

Probes:

a. What precipitated the crisis?

b. How else could it have been handled?

c. What did the emotional response of the teacher mean to the student? (See Nelson-Barber commentary.)

d. Why did the parent respond positively?

e. What were the risks for the teacher in her emotional display?

5. What changed for the student and teacher?

Probes:

a. Why was the teacher able to reach Mario? (Discuss Pringle's commentary on the "window.")

b. What aspects of cultural adaptation was the teacher assisting in this case?

c. What new perspectives did Mario's mother develop about the school?

d. How was Mario able to improve as a result of the teacher's intervention?

e. What were shared cultural experiences between the teacher and student?

f. What were the cultural differences between the student and teacher?

6. Discuss the meaning of the balance between academic hopes, preparing for success in U.S. culture, and supporting family values and home culture. (Refer to Pringle's commentary.)

Probes:

a. Are students pulled by expectations? How?

b. How can the teacher and school help the student balance these worlds?

7. Are there any principles you can generate from this special setting that would be helpful for regular classrooms?

My "Good Year" Explodes: A Confrontation with Parents

This case has many layers. Unlike most of the other cases in this book, the problems at issue here are not specific to diverse settings; they could happen in any school where parents are active players. The case is particularly timely in this era of emphasis on site-based management and parent involvement. Discussions about the best curricula and teaching methods are bound to create tension.

On the surface, the case is about a Japanese-American teacher's shock at receiving a hand-delivered letter, signed by a group of her students' parents, requesting that their children be placed in a different teacher's classroom for the following year. Apparently, the parents disapproved of the way she taught mathematics and thought their children would not progress appropriately. They wanted their children to spend more time on rote memorization, drill, and practice.

The teacher does not understand why the parents disapproved so strongly. Her students' math scores on the California Test of Basic Skills showed satisfactory progress. She and many other faculty members had worked hard to learn progressive strategies that made mathematics more meaningful. Moreover, the parents had numerous opportunities to communicate concern — at back-to-school night, in written communications, and during their volunteer days in her classroom — but no one had ever expressed disapproval. Why wait until the end of the year to show concern? Why go to the extreme measure of simultaneously sending the letter to the principal, the district office, and the school board? In short, what had this teacher done wrong? And how should she handle future disagreements with parents?

This case deals with many issues: faculty versus parent control, mathematics teaching methods, hurt feelings, and cultural norms of criticism. The five commentaries are particularly instructive because they represent the perspectives of: 1) a well-known education historian, who helps us see these parents' actions in the context of parent roles at other points in history; 2) another teacher in the same school; 3) a mathematics educator, who

questions how new teaching methods are being applied in classrooms; 4) a Japanese-American staff developer, who offers a cultural interpretation of what occurred; and 5) an administrator.

CONTEXT

This is a Japanese bilingual, bi-cultural school whose reputation as one of the district's finest schools is due to its dedicated staff and links to the community. The parent group actively raises funds, participates in classrooms, and is an integral part of decision making in all aspects of school life.

Though the school is dominated by Japanese-Americans, half of whom are immigrants, many Caucasian parents also try to enroll their children. As one of the commentators noted, the parents have a great stake in their children's education and form an external network of communication. But their norms of communication — among one another and with the faculty — may vary along cultural paths.

SEGMENTS OF THE DISCUSSION

It may be appropriate to begin this session with some background about two sometimes conflicting issues in education today: major curricular reform and increased parent involvement via site-based management. Discussions about what and how to teach are bound to create tensions — when both parents and teachers have strong opinions and major investments in each. As stated above, the problems such tensions raised in this case could happen in any school where parents are actively involved.

To begin the case discussion, ask, "What are the facts of this case?" Probe for understanding of: the context; what actually happened; how the teacher felt; the apparent reasons for parent discontent; and the response of the faculty.

What do we know about the teacher? The teacher is a Japanese-American woman known among her colleagues as outstanding and dedicated. She has attended numerous workshops to improve her teaching of mathematics and cites evidence that the time was well spent. Her students appeared more motivated and challenged, and they had performed well on the California Test of Basic Skills. Thus, she was shocked and terribly hurt by the parents' letter:

> My pride and dignity had been wounded when my professionalism and integrity were questioned. Worse, I had been accused of doing a disservice to the children. I was haunted by thoughts that I had brought this on myself, and I was full of guilt.

A cultural influence. It's interesting that the teacher comes from the same ethnic group as most of her students, yet seems surprised that she got no hint of negative parental reaction to her teaching. Several commentators note that Asian parents, as a group, may have a difficult time communicating disapproval because of their norm of respect for classroom teachers and concern for "face." Moreover, "generalized parental fears about negatively affecting a teacher's attitude toward their child" probably added to their hesitation to confront the teacher with their concerns. It is not surprising, then, that the parents in this teacher's class never voiced their disapproval, even though they had many opportunities to do so.

In her commentary Hiroshima wonders why the parents did not go individually to the principal about having their child removed, which would have saved embarrassment on the part of both the teacher and the parents. Their decision to deliver a letter that caused the teacher to "lose face," raises questions about who may have been the instigator. The norm of communication among whites tends to be more direct than among Japanese-Americans.

The faculty's response. What was the faculty response to the teacher's situation? The case briefly describes a set of procedures that the faculty developed as a result of the parents' actions. But Garfield's commentary, which takes the perspective of another faculty member who also felt "attacked" by the parents' actions, gives a more complete picture of the teachers' reactions.

The parents' response: Curriculum questions. It is easy for readers of this case to empathize with the teachers' sense of betrayal and frustration with the parental intrusion on their mathematics instruction. According to the narrative and some commentaries, this teacher and others on the faculty spent a great deal of time going to workshops to learn how to incorporate techniques from the newly mandated California State Mathematics Framework. As a result, they firmly believed that what they were taught represented the best possible form of mathematics instruction.

But Barnett's commentary raises some valid questions. While not criticizing this particular teacher, Barnett asks whether the parents may have had a legitimate concern. The current national movement in mathematics education de-emphasizes rote drill and practice and puts a stronger emphasis on thinking and understanding. But it is possible for teachers to go to workshops — with good intentions about learning new ideas — and return to their classrooms without comprehending how to apply the concepts in ways that promote thinking and understanding.

Isn't it possible that parents watching their children struggle to solve mathematical problems may find that their children lack the understanding to solve the problems? Barnett suggests that we must be open to parents' concerns about their children's instruction, because they may know more than the teachers about how their children learn.

Movement toward site-based management. This case is also significant because of the current movement toward site-based management. Many districts are finding that faculty-community teams organized to improve school governance and decision making can run into unanticipated difficulties. As Jimenez says in his commentary, "there may be an inherent tension between the parents' desire for the best schooling for their child and the school professional's attempt to create the most nurturing, challenging, and coherent program for all students." Jimenez's analysis of problems created by school bureaucracy and differing cultural norms illuminates these issues.

Cuban also comments on some of the cultural barriers that might surround parent/teacher conflicts. As he says in his analysis, "The usual ways that a teacher and school tell culturally diverse parents what their children are learning and how they learn it often fails to convey what is intended. . . Bureaucratic solutions arrived at by the school community could squelch rather than encourage parent input about what is appropriate for their children."

What are some ways to constructively resolve curriculum disagreements between teachers and parents? When there are differences, what's the bottom line? What should be the respective roles of parents and teachers in determining how to best teach their children?

Closing the Discussion

The questions raised by this case cannot be "answered" in a case discussion. Such problems will be resolved differently at each school where they occur. That said, one way to close this discussion is to synthesize the key issues and unanswered questions raised by the group. Then ask participants to generate principles that may help resolve faculty-teacher confrontations.

Suggested Discussion Outline

1. What were the facts of the case?

   Probes:

   a. What do we know about the ethnic mix of the school?

   b. Why was the teacher feeling good at the end of the year?

   c. What was the reason for the parents' discontent?

   d. How did the teacher frame the problems?

   e. What was the response of the rest of the faculty to this teacher's dilemma?

2. What do we know about the teacher in this case?

   Probes:

   a. Was she a good teacher? How do we know?

   b. What kind of educative activities does she engage in to improve her teaching?

   c. What is the relationship between this teacher and the rest of her faculty?

   d. What was her ethnic background?

   e. How does "loss of face" influence her response to the situation?

3. What do we know about most of the parents in this case?

   Probes:

   a. What is the dominant ethnic group?

b. What generalities mark Japanese norms of communication? What may we expect?

c. From which ethnic group is the PTA President? What difference might this make?

d. How does the PTA's active involvement in the school influence this case?

4. Why do you think the parents chose to communicate with the teacher by way of a signed letter?

Probes:

a. How do different norms of communication influence this case?

b. What are some organizational and/or bureaucratic constraints?

c. How do such constraints influence the development of a trusting relationship between parents and teachers?

5. Does the faculty response to this dilemma promote a climate of trust between faculty and parents? (Refer to Cuban's and Jimenez's commentary.)

Probe:

a. What do the "grievance procedures" communicate to parents?

6. Why do you think the parents disapproved of the curriculum?

Probes:

a. Is there a possibility that the parents had a legitimate concern? (Refer to Barnett's commentary.)

b. What may the parents know about the ways their children learn that teachers may not be aware of?

7. From the students' perspective, what are the difficulties of this situation?

8. What can teachers do to help their students mediate the opposing expectations of their parents and teachers?

Probe:

a. What do you do?

9. What are some alternate strategies that this teacher, principal, and faculty could consider to increase the trust between parents and teachers?

Probes:

a. What can teachers do to develop better working relationships with parents?

b. What could this teacher have done to prevent this situation?

c. What are the risks and consequences of each strategy?

10. What are some general strategies that a school could develop that would both increase the trust between parents and teachers and reduce the barriers of communication?

Probe:

a. What are the risks and consequences for each strategy?

11. When there are differences between parents and teachers, what's the bottom line? What should be the respective roles of parents and teachers in determining how to best teach their children?

    Probes:

    a. What are the consequences for the students?

    b. What are the consequences for the ethos of the school?

12. In summary, what are the key issues and unanswered questions that arose from this case discussion?

13. Are there any principles that we can generate that should be considered for resolving future faculty-teacher confrontations?

Opening Pandora's Box: The Mystery Behind an "Ideal Student"

The story begins when one eager and helpful Chinese-American girl develops an obsessive friendship with another. The teacher is baffled by disruptions that occur as the friendship ends. In the course of trying to help the troubled young student, the teacher learns a great deal about the child's family relationships. A series of explosive conflicts is followed by the teacher's attempt to draw the parents into a dialogue about the girl's problems. The teacher is alarmed by the emotional problems she sees, yet she fails to involve the parents — perhaps because of psychological or cultural barriers between the family and the school. The family manages to smooth over the problems and distance itself from the teacher. Sadly, the teacher senses that the student's resumption of her previous ideal behavior may only be temporary; exemplary behavior may be her mechanism for coping with serious personal and family issues.

CONTEXT

The cultural underpinnings of this case can only be described in the most general way, since Chinese and Chinese-American families are culturally heterogeneous. But as the commentaries suggest, such families do show some predictable characteristics: unequal treatment of boys and girls related to patriarchal Chinese traditions; protection of private family information from public scrutiny; and a valuing of discipline, restraint, obedience, and authority.

We know little of the family's migration from China or of their familiarity with the American school system. The degree of their disruption may have affected their perceptions and sense of trust for school authorities. Their experiences with racial discrimination, English language difficulties, and family histories may complicate their involvement with school staff. It is important to explore the school's and teacher's assumptions about the way parents should be involved and how it contrasts with Chinese-American attitudes about parent participation. We do know that the family in this case has main-tained close ties to their home in Hong Kong and that they are themselves limited-English speakers. It is clear that they value their language and culture; Connie continues to attend Chinese school three days a week.

In many Chinese-American communities, school and community relationships are distant, and the role of the teacher is quite idealized. We don't have a clear picture of this family's feelings about the teacher's interventions. Given that traditional cultures associate authority with age, it might be important to explore how the parents responded to the conference when Connie was brought in. The cultural context of this case also makes it difficult for us to sort out the psychological meaning of Connie's behavior. Even such simple things as the cultural attitude toward pets and toward friendships outside the family and neighborhood play a part.

The other students involved in the situation are also Chinese-American immigrant girls, yet their behavior is different from Connie's, indicating that her responses may go beyond a cultural norm. Even Connie's mother reflects on whether her daughter's behavior is "normal." In other words, psychopathological issues can often be obscured by a search for cultural clues to explain behavior. We have few Chinese-American school psychologists and psychometricians to provide us the knowledge and tools for adequately assessing why a student is acting out. What is clear is that this teacher was ill-equipped to know what would have been a cultural norm in this setting and what would have constituted a more significant individual and family disturbance. Nelson-Barber's commentary provides insights into these issues.

SEGMENTS OF THE DISCUSSION

The discussion should go beyond the level of teacher intervention and student response. The group should extensively explore the role that parents, family, and culture play in a student's school success.

What do we know about the teacher? This experienced teacher has just changed schools; she may not know the community and school that well. Though she is white, she is comfortable with her immigrant students. At several critical points in the story, she saw red warning flags. She describes a gut-level sense of alarm even though her principal feels she has overreacted. Throughout the case, the teacher senses hidden family problems. There is a discrepancy between the family's response to Connie's situation and the teacher's deep concern. We know that the teacher regarded this situation as serious.

Facilitators may want to examine how the teacher could have gotten more information. How might she have learned more about the family? Why didn't she get expert help from a school psychologist or a culturally knowledgeable counselor? What other possibilities for intervention could have been explored beyond the teacher's talks with student and family? What would have been the risks and consequences of referring this student and family to counseling?

What do we know about the family? This appears to be a traditional Chinese family with strong cultural bonds demonstrated by their frequent visits to Hong Kong and their emphasis on a Chinese school for Connie. We know they are working class because they have Connie in the school's low-income based day care. It is important to consider what the parents may have thought about the teacher's interventions. Clearly, they believed that discipline was important in handling Connie's acting out. Even her suicide threat led to a spanking. Her outbursts at the parent conference led to restraint and control. We wonder if the parents' responses were culturally governed by values of authority and discipline. What were the gender issues, with boys favored over girls? How did the parents react to the teacher's demonstrative hug and understanding acceptance of Connie's emotional display? Nelson-Barber's commentary on authority and obedience gives us insight on these cultural issues.

Parent-teacher encounter. The teacher's inability to reach the parents may have had something to do with the cultural misunderstandings between them. How was Connie's referral to the principal viewed by the parents? What was the significance of bringing Connie into the parent conference? Differences in values about directness, openness, styles of communication and sharing of family information between the teacher and the parents may have come into play. In particular, the differences in the teacher's interpersonal style and the parents' restraint create a competing set of messages for Connie. Nelson-Barber's commentary targets the important issue of communicating across differences.

What do we know about the student? We know that Connie spends a great deal of time in an institutional setting away from her parents. Her earlier suicide threat indicates that she has been trying to get her parents' attention for some time. Both the excessive need for a friend and her obsessive response to her pet's loss reveal a child whose emotional needs are not being met. In a developmental sense, her constant focus on her best friend is in keeping with same-sex attachments common to girls in puberty, despite the mother's fear that it isn't normal. Could the teacher have been more effective at helping the girl gain her parents' understanding of her deep needs?

Teachers at high schools with large Chinese populations have observed that the high standards, unrealistic expectations, and unresponsive emotional settings common to Chinese-American students can cause even overachieving students to feel depressed and hopeless. We might also note Connie's own concern about her brother's favored position, indicative of gender roles in traditional Chinese cultures.

Connie's outbursts. As the story progresses, Connie's behaviors reveal that her emotional disturbances have a long history. Her intense friendship is marked by anger and jealousy. Her jealousy over her parents' treatment of her brother Martin seems to feed a deep rage that surfaces in the parent-teacher encounter. Despite the strong cultural taboos against defying parents, Connie exploded in response to her mother's caution about friendship. Lilly Siu points out in her commentary that the issue of second-class status for girls in Chinese culture is very real, but even she acknowledges the seriousness of Connie's psychological problems.

Connie's behavior may be a response to both cultural practices and unmet personal needs. Yet, we sense that the teacher's emotional and caring support for Connie is not sufficient to fill the deficits at home and may even have created new conflicts and pressures, if Connie feels caught between teacher and parent expectations.

CLOSING THE DISCUSSION

It is important to synthesize what we learned about the family and its role during critical moments in the case. Discussing what the characters might have thought about key incidents even when the story doesn't reveal their attitudes helps us to frame this case as a school-community problem as well as a story about a teacher-student relationship.

SUGGESTED DISCUSSION OUTLINE

1. What were the most important issues in this case?

    Probes:

    a. Cultural?

    b. Gender-related?

    c. Instructional?

    d. Familial?

    e. Psychological?

2. The student's behavior changed drastically. What triggered this?

    Probes:

    a. How could the situation have been handled differently?

    b. What part did the parents play in the behavior change?

3. The teacher's first intervention outside the classroom was to send the girls to the principal's office.

    Probes:

    a. How was this viewed?

    b. Why didn't it work?

    c. What were the risks and consequences of this decision?

4. Describe the parent encounter. What were key points, key information given?

    Probes:

    a. List some of the cultural issues, differences, or conflicts that were present in the teacher-parent exchange. (See Nelson-Barber commentary.)

    b. What could have been done to enlist the parents' support?

    c. What might have happened if Connie hadn't participated in the conference?

5. What did Connie feel about the situation?

    Probes:

    a. About her teacher's help?

    b. About her parents' response?

    c. About her family situation? (See Siu commentary.)

d. What did she expect or need from the teacher?

e. Discuss her response to competing messages from teacher and parents.

6. What made the teacher most uncomfortable in this situation?

    Probes:

    a. What was she afraid of?

    b. Why didn't she seek counseling assistance?

    c. What was she trying to accomplish for Connie? For the family? For herself?

    d. How did her communication style and values differ from the family?

7. At one point, the teacher attempts to convince the principal that this is a very serious situation (the suicide gesture), but the principal doesn't intervene. Why?

    Probes:

    a. What could have contributed to the principal's apparent lack of concern?

    b. What could the teacher have done at this point?

8. Why did Connie apologize to the teacher?

    Probes:

    a. What did it reflect about family and cultural values?

    b. How could the teacher have responded?

    c. How did Connie feel about it?

9. What other incidents or details make us think that things are not resolved with Connie, with her parents?

    Probes:

    a. What can we predict might happen to Connie in the years ahead?

    b. What do we think troubles the teacher most?

10. In the largest sense, what were the individual, familial, and cultural issues at play in this case?

    Probes:

    a. What could the teacher have done to maintain trust with the student and parents?

    b. Was there a values conflict between home and school?

    c. What gender/culture issues came into play? How would the case have differed if the central character had been a boy?

    d. What were the key points of rupture?

    e. What alternative interventions could the teacher have made? What would have been the risks and consequences of the intervention?

11. What have you learned from this case?

    Probes:

    a. What is the most important cultural knowledge you gained?

    b. What guiding principles came from this case?

This case begins when 15 students who were supposed to participate in a volunteer-sponsored arts program didn't show up. All lived in the same housing project. Though the faculty had warned the volunteers that they should send a bus to transport the students across the city for the performance, the volunteers ignored the warning because they felt sure the parents wouldn't let their children miss "so important an opportunity." As time grew short, they realized they were wrong. They called this teacher-author to see if she could do anything to get the children to the park.

The rest of the case describes how and why the teacher was successful. In particular, the case illustrates the importance of establishing immediate and ongoing contact with students' families and lays some important ground rules for establishing those contacts. It also shows why it is so critical for an inner-city teacher to play a larger than normal role in his or her students' lives.

The author wrote this case because of her passionate belief in home contacts. As she said to the editors, "One of the problems in inner-city schools is that many teachers don't know how to reach out beyond the classroom into the personal lives of their students." While acknowledging the dangers of going into certain locales, she is convinced that careful preparation and sustained contact can defuse most risky situations.

The commentators react to this case from two very different perspectives. A white teacher illustrates that one does not have to be a teacher of color to develop meaningful personal relationships with students of color and their families. We then read about the importance of such relationships from the viewpoint of an educational anthropologist.

CONTEXT

This case takes place in a large urban school where many students are bused in from a housing project located in another part of the city. Though similar busing arrange-

ments are common in urban areas and have many advantages, one problem is a marked decrease in parent participation and involvement. Some teachers conclude that these parents stay away from school because they simply don't care about their children's education. In fact they may care intensely but are hampered from participating by a number of factors. Most families who live in project housing are headed by single mothers or grandmothers with very limited resources. They may not have the money to pay for baby-sitters so they can leave or for bus fare to get to the school. Others may have work schedules that prohibit trips across the city.

SEGMENTS OF THE DISCUSSION

The arts program. Though the author intended to focus attention on the importance of initiating contacts with families, the discussion should begin by exploring the surface problem: Why didn't the youngsters show up for the performance? Some readers — particularly middle-class teachers who have had little or no prior experience with poor families in diverse settings — may be as baffled as the school volunteers. In their experience, such performances are very important events in the lives of children and their families, particularly when the location is a prestigious public place. For these readers, the case could confirm the stereotype that parents in projects simply don't care about their children's education.

The parents' perspective. This discussion can be an interesting assessment of the participants' sensitivity to and experience with diverse communities. The facilitator should guide the group to examine the dilemma from the parents' perspective. If participants cannot come up with some rationales that make sense, you might try reframing the problem with a question like this: Why might these parents be reluctant to send their children to participate in an outdoor event? Responses may include any of the following: 1) most households are run by single mothers or grandmothers who have other responsibilities and cannot come to the performance; 2) parents do not want to send their children unattended on a bus; 3) parents are uncomfortable sending their children to an alien neighborhood unchaperoned; 4) parents may neither know nor trust the persons in charge; and 5) the children may not have told their parent(s) that the activity was important to them. This discussion may stimulate participants to remember their own fears about going to an alien neighborhood.

The event itself. It is important to emphasize that this arts event was organized and directed by school volunteers, not the teacher-author. Though the teacher and other faculty had predicted that the children would not show up unless arrangements were made for their transportation, the teachers could not control the situation.

Why make home visits? A large part of the discussion should focus on why home visits are so important to the students and families in inner-city schools. As Nelson-Barber points out in her commentary, it is becoming increasingly evident that, in many urban centers, effective teaching often means going beyond the traditional conception of "content to be taught." Many educators claim that success often depends on a teacher's ability to both forge meaningful relationships with their students and draw on local values and expectations about teaching and learning. The skills of attending to students' broader social and familial contexts often cannot be honed within the confines of a classroom or a school.

The teacher-author makes a strong case for initiating home contacts during the first few weeks of school. Those interactions, she feels, need to be positive experiences, since they lay the foundation for resolving problems that might occur later on in the school year. Direct involvement is meaningful to families who "feel ignored or believe that they have little voice in the educational decisions for their children" (Nelson-Barber's commentary). It also increases a teacher's understanding of her students' behavior and her capacity to handle a disruptive child.

How to initiate contact. This teacher offers some ground rules for initiating contact with families who live in housing projects. These may be particularly helpful to teachers who have little experience with such settings. Sensitivity to the local norms of behavior can make or break the success of any visit (note especially the author's account of going to a student's home to discuss a theft, then changing her plans when she met her student's great grandmother). It also lowers the risk of being at the right place at the wrong time, such as the author's description of "the classic robbery setup."

The author makes particular reference to the importance of the "Power Mom" or "Grandma," as she is often called, in predominantly African-American settings. Such older women have been a source of information and inspiration for many educators. The importance of women's roles in black communities can be traced to the historic position of women in the Baptist church, the socio-economic conditions that produce predominantly female, single-parent households, and the child-rearing practices that occur in extended families.

Should direct home contact be part of a teacher's role? What is the role of a teacher? Should direct home contact be included in that role? Some participants, especially secondary teachers, who often teach over 100 students, argue that teachers can only be expected to teach content and that personal contact with students and families cannot be part of the role of teachers. While this description may fit the traditional concept of a teacher, the purpose of this case discussion is to encourage teachers to think more broadly. A current movement among many educators (e.g., James Comer) calls for school restructuring that enables teachers to reach beyond their own classrooms and into the personal lives of their students and families. This is particularly important in inner-city settings, where parental involvement and support cannot be taken for granted.

This concept of effective teaching is more time consuming than the traditional image. Discussions about what outreach is or can be, and how much can be done without burning out are important. New teachers in particular may be overwhelmed with setting up new curricula and will need support as they learn to set priorities.

Some teachers may argue that visiting certain housing projects is too dangerous, and that minority parents will be more accepting of minority teachers than of whites. Others don't give up so easily. One of the commentators, Joan Tibbetts, is a white teacher who wrote her own mini-case about how she established tutoring services in the projects with parental support. Both Tibbetts and the case author maintain that successful home visits depend on how these contacts are established and nurtured.

CLOSING THE DISCUSSION

Participants should be encouraged to share their own experiences about the advantages of establishing home contacts. At the end of the discussion, it may be useful to generate a list of both new insights and unanswered questions that were stimulated by the case analysis.

SUGGESTED DISCUSSION OUTLINE

1. What were the facts of this case?

2. Why do you think the students didn't show up for the performance?

    Probes:

    a. Why might the students' parent[s] hesitate to send them to the performance?

    b. Why might the students be reluctant to participate in the performance?

3. The author makes a case for the importance of making direct contact with students' families early in the year. Do you agree?

Probes:

a. How much can we assume we can accomplish merely within the walls of our classrooms?

b. What are the ramifications of busing and single-parent households for parent participation in schools?

c. What are the realistic differences between what can be accomplished by elementary versus secondary teachers?

4. What are some of the strategies that the author used for making home contacts?

    Probes:

    a. What were the risks and consequences of each strategy?

    b. How did the author demonstrate sensitivity to the norms of behavior of the families (grandmother)?

5. What are some alternate strategies for making contact with your students' families?

    Probe:

    a. What are some of the risks and consequences of each one?

6. How do you think the parents in this case viewed the school?

    Probes:

    a. Do they trust the teachers? Why?

    b. Do they value their children's education? How would we know?

c. What might prevent parents from becoming involved in their children's school activities and/or parent conferences?

7. Do you establish contact with your students' families? If yes:

    Probes:

    a. What do you do?

    b. Of what value are these contacts?

    c. What might prevent you from making contacts with parents?

    d. Of what value are home visits?

8. Are there any principles that we can generate on the importance of and methods for making direct home contacts? Do you have any new insights and/or unanswered questions that were stimulated by the case analysis?

APPENDIX A

Dealing With Interpersonal Resistance

The key to understanding the nature of resistance is to realize that it is a reaction to an emotional process taking place within an individual.

Resistance is a predictable, natural, emotional reaction against the process of being helped and against the process of having to face up to difficult problems.

The skill in dealing with interpersonal resistance is:

1. to be able to identify when resistance is occurring.

2. to view resistance as a natural process and a sign that you are on target.

3. to support the other person in expressing the resistance directly.

4. to not take the expression of the resistance personally or as an attack upon you or your competence.

Some common forms of interpersonal resistance are:

1. remaining silent.

2. requesting more and more specifics.

3. giving more and more details without being asked.

4. changing the subject frequently.

5. maintaining that there is not enough time to deal with the problem.

6. emphasizing the impracticality of what is being suggested.

7. stressing that what is being said comes as no surprise.

8. attacking one's competence, credentials, or credibility.

9. expressing confusion or lack of understanding in a repeated manner.

10. intellectualizing or moving into academic abstractions.

11. agreeing with everything that is being said without questioning it.

12. stating that the problem seems to be going away or resolving itself.

13. denying any ownership in a problem or any responsibility for its solution.

When you encounter resistance, you are seeing the surface expression of more underlying anxieties. Two things are happening:

1. the person is feeling uncomfortable, and

2. the person is expressing the discomfort indirectly.

The direct expression of underlying concerns is not resistance. Resistance only occurs when the concerns about facing difficult realities and the choice not to deal with them are expressed indirectly.

Most expressions of resistance stem from an individual's:

1. concerns about control.

2. concerns about vulnerability.

There is no way you can talk another person out of his/her resistance, because resistance is an emotional process. Behind the resistance are certain feelings. You cannot talk people out of how they are feeling.

Feelings pass and change when they get expressed directly.

The Basic Steps for Handling Interpersonal Resistance Are:

1. Physically move closer to the hostile participant.

2. Make direct eye contact.

3. Identify in your own mind what form the resistance is taking. The skill is to pick up the cues from the other person and then, in your head, to put some words on what you see happening.

4. State, in a neutral, non-punishing way, the form the resistance is taking. This is called "naming the resistance." The skill is to find neutral language.

5. Be quiet. Allow the other person to respond to your statement about the resistance.

6. Courteously solicit information about the nature of their protest.

7. Dialogue in a positive and supportive way about their concerns.

How to Listen to the Resister:

1. Remain neutral.

   Do not give advice, agree or disagree, criticize or interrupt.

2. Give your complete attention.

   Let him know you are listening. Nod your head — "Uh, huh, I see what you mean."

3. Ask about his statements.

   Dig out information, invite him to tell everything. Say, "In addition to that is there anything else?"

4. Restate his main points.

   Let him hear the exact words restated by you. This prompts him to stick to the facts and to think intelligently.

5. Put his feelings into words.

   State what his feelings seem to be. When he hears them voiced by you he evaluates and tempers them.

6. Get agreement.

   Summarize what you have both said — encourage him to suggest the next step or course of action.

How to Ask Questions of the Resister:

1. No third degree.

   Use questions to help the other person think — never to degrade or to spy.

2. Ask "W" questions.

   What, Why, When, Where, Who, and How are the key words that will secure facts and information.

3. Ask questions that make him go deeper.

Ask for evidence, examples or explanations to discover reasons behind his thinking.

4. Ask "suppose" questions.

   Introduce a new idea, break a deadlock or bring up an overlooked point with: "Suppose we. . .?"

5. Ask him.

   To encourage others to think or to avoid committing yourself, return the question or relay it to another qualified person.

6. Ask questions that get agreement.

   Offer several solutions in the form of a question.

Adapted from:

Block, Peter. (1981). *Flawless Consulting: A Guide to Getting Your Expertise Used*, pp. 1-139. Austin, TX: Learning Concepts.

Pickhardt, Carl E. (1980). "Participant Hostility: Why It Comes With the Territory," *Training, 17*(9), pp. 16, 19-20.

APPENDIX B

Active Listening

There are two components of active listening. They are:

1. Attending

   Focus on the speaker. Attend to:

   - the total meaning of the message

     - what he or she says (content)

     - how he or she says it (feeling and attitudes underlying the content)

   - the nonverbal behaviors/cues

2. Reflecting

   - Reflect in words and body language what the speaker is communicating.

   - Reflect the feelings the speaker is expressing in the total communication.

   - Communicate genuine acceptance of the person and his feelings.

What to avoid:

   - Pleading, reasoning, scolding, insulting, prodding— any actions which stand in the way of listening with understanding. This is the most potent agent of change.

   - Decisions, judgments, and evaluations — these actions convey that we are thinking for people rather than *with* them.

Pitfalls in Active Listening

   - The personal risk

     - It takes great inner security and courage to risk self in understanding another.

   - The "constant refrain"

     - Mechanical "parroting" of content is not active listening.

   - Timing

     - When someone is asking for factual information or when there is no time to deal with the situation, do not use active listening.

   - Emotional danger signals

     - Defensiveness: When we find ourselves emphasizing a point or trying to convince another, emotions are high and we may be less able to listen.

     - Resentment of opposition: an opposing view may stand in the way of our listening.

   - Listening to ourselves

     - This is a prerequisite of listening to others. We need to be sure of our own position, values, and needs.

Benefits of Active Listening

   - It communicates acceptance and increases interpersonal trust.

   - It facilitates problem solving.

- It establishes a nurturing climate which tends to build self-esteem.

———————————————

Adapted from:

The Community Board Program. (1990). *Starting a Conflict Managers Program,* pp. 10-15. San Francisco: Author. Used with permission.

62   69